How to Make Audio Drama

How to Make Audio Drama:
A Guide to Fiction Podcasting

By Tal Minear

ISBN: 979-8-9950618-0-9 (Paperback)

ISBN: 979-8-9950618-1-6 (Hardcover)

ISBN: 979-8-9950618-2-3 (E-book)

Library of Congress Control Number: 2026905254

Printed in the United States of America.

First Printing, 2026.

Editing by Wil Williams.

Front cover design by Tal Minear.

Book formatted by Tal Minear.

www.talminear.com

To our inner whimsy.

Table of Contents

Chapter 1

You Can Make an Audio Drama

I'm sitting like a shrimp at my desk, staring at my laptop. There are many windows open on the screen:

- A PDF file with the script.
- A couple File Explorer folders - one for the episode, three for different SFX searches, and something unrelated I forgot to close.
- Firefox is open with too many tabs - Freesound, Dropbox, Google Drive…
- There's a Discord window somewhere, too.

But in front of everything is Adobe Audition, which has frozen. I try to remember the last time I saved the episode. It was too long ago. I debate between letting it buffer and force closing the program. Miraculously, it unfreezes. I sigh with relief and immediately save my work.

When I hit play, my world will come to life, and all of this will have been worth it.

What is an Audio Drama?

Audio Dramas have many names, including "Radio Plays," "Fiction Podcasts," "Audio Theater," and many combinations thereof (such as "Audio Fiction"). The Radio Play was a popular form of entertainment pre-television.

Here in America, the best known one was *War of the Worlds* in 1938. Across the pond, the BBC produces more hits than I can name. With the popularization of podcasting in the 2010s, the medium of Audio Theater became more accessible to the individual. Anyone could publish a fiction podcast, and many did.

People from all walks of life make audio dramas. As you'd expect, plenty of them come from the arts. Some people pivot to fiction podcasting from TV or movie production, while others arrive from theater or novels or poetry. But there are also IT techs, engineers, and scientists making audio dramas. There are graphic designers, managers, musicians, and more. I've listened to shows created by high school students and shows created by people older than my parents. I've met and worked with producers across the globe. This variety of life experience is reflected in the variety of fiction podcasts out there.

My History in Audio Drama

I've been making audio dramas for over 7 years. My favorite genre to work in is fantasy, but I've also created slice of life, sci-fi, and horror podcasts. I'll be using examples from the shows I've produced throughout this book, including:

- *Sidequesting*
- *What Will Be Here?*
- *Someone Dies In This Elevator*
- *Re: Dracula*
- *Re: Carmilla*
- *Re: Frankenstein*

- *Joy to the World*
- *Of The Sword*
- *Falling Forward*
- *Hubris: A 24 Hour Podcast Project*
- *Pilot Light*

I find myself drawn to making limited series, because I love playing in different worlds. My favorite part of audio drama production is sound design, so I usually (but not always) do the sound design on audio dramas I produce. I'm often writing and voice acting in them too.

Outside of the podcasts I produce, I've been a voice actor in almost 100 different audio dramas, a sound designer for about ten other productions, and a guest writer for a few. My work has been featured in The *Atlantic*, The *New York Times*, and *Vogue*. My podcasts have been an official selection of over 20 film and web fests, with multiple award wins. My most popular audio drama, *Re: Dracula*, has over 2 million downloads and was featured in Tumblr's 2023 and 2024 Year in Review wrap ups. In 2024, I received the William Dufris Achievement Award for excellence in audio fiction at the New Jersey Web Fest Gala.

Making audio drama is my favorite hobby because it's so many different things rolled up in one. I've created watercolor paintings for cover art. I've produced an entire concept album for a show. I've written so many different stories, long and short, for so many different genres. I taught myself sound design. I learned voice acting. I got really good at project management. The list goes on and on.

You might want to make an audio drama because you too like doing many different things. Or perhaps you have a story in your head that you need to get out in the world. Maybe the idea of working with actors and sound designers to bring your vision to life is what's drawn you to this medium. Or you might have another reason! There are many to choose from!

Everybody starts somewhere. For me, that place was called "winging it." Sometimes I feel like I am still winging it . . . but I've learned a LOT. I love working with other creators and helping new showrunners find their way. I also really want podcasting to be more accessible. As part of that effort, I've been writing how-to articles and sharing resources since I found out people wanted to read them. This book is the cumulation of that work and knowledge.

It's Time to Dive In

I wanted everything I've learned to live in one easy-to-find place, so that it's easy to share it all. I'm assuming some familiarity with the medium (you've listened to an audio drama before, right?), but I'm not assuming any familiarity with *making* audio drama. If you're here to figure out where to start, you won't get lost between the pages.

This book focuses on *indie* audio drama production, meaning production that doesn't include any outside funding or help from a company or network. It's kind of like self-publishing a book. Indie audio drama doesn't need approval from an agent or publishing house (or anyone, really) to reach an audience. You can make it yourself and get it to listeners without an intermediary.

In this book, we'll be exploring the role of a showrunner in depth (that's you, the runner of your show!). I will touch on other parts of audio drama production, like acting, directing, and audio editing more generally. Showrunners frequently take on these roles, but I won't be teaching you how to become a top-notch actor, director, or sound designer. Instead, I'll explain the basics of what you should keep in mind when doing these roles for the first time as part of an audio drama.

This is not a technical guide, but rather a *production* guide. The technology behind podcasting is ever-growing and ever-changing. The best practices for working in a DAW (digital audio workstation), the best microphones to use, the best hosting services for an RSS feed . . . it gets outdated quickly. We'll be covering more evergreen topics, like knowing what stories work best in audio, how to cast your show, and where to start when marketing it. For technical help, I recommend turning to the internet or fellow audio creators.

At the end of this book, you'll feel more prepared to be an audio drama producer, be able to make a better podcast, and know where to look for even more help. You'll learn the basic concepts of all the roles involved in audio drama production, either to use as a jumping-off point to learn more or to collaborate with others who are well versed in the roles. You'll also get some advice on the more philosophical aspects of audio drama creation, such as why to start one or when to end it.

I assume you picked this book up because you're interested in making an audio drama (or fiction podcast, or radio play, or whatever the cool kids are calling it these days). Maybe you've started, but are floundering before the finish line. Or perhaps you're wondering if this is something you even can do. Maybe you just want to learn more about something you think is cool. Whatever it is, I hope by the end of this book, you'll know that you CAN make an audio drama!

Chapter 2
Starting With an Idea

The Power of Audio

Here are some questions you should have answers to before you start working on your audio drama:

Why audio drama? What about your show concept makes it well suited for this medium?

You could self-publish a book, start a web series, or write a play. Know what's drawing you to audio drama, and specifically what's drawing you to audio drama *with this idea*. If you've got multiple ideas, you should start with the one that works best in the audio drama format (to figure that out, stay tuned for the next section).

What is your goal? What would you define as a successful show?

Perhaps you're happy just to finish the pilot, a whole season, or bring the story to its natural end. Maybe you want to hit a certain download milestone, or amass a specific follower count on the podcast social media page. Your goal might be to win an award at a festival, or get your work featured in the press. You might want to make money from the podcast, or just break even on show expenses. Maybe you want to collaborate with specific people, land on a certain network, or speak at a podcast event. Maybe your goal is a TV or novel adaptation. Everyone's idea of success is different. If you know going into it what you want out of it, you'll be able to focus on bringing your goals to life.

Is this a hobby, or do you want to be professional?

The low barrier to publication means that low-budget indie shows regularly chart next to professionally produced, high budget shows. This means that an audio drama you make could land in the top 100 podcasts for your country, right next to a show with A-list celebrities in the cast. If a podcast sounds good, listeners don't care who made it, which leads to a nebulous space full of bickering about what *really* makes a show indie. There's not actually distinct lines between "hobby," "indie," and "professional." We'll explore these definitions more later. For now, have an idea of how much money you can spend on your audio drama, and if you want to someday do it for a living. This will help you decide how to proceed with different aspects of production.

But that's not all! Ideally, before you start writing your audio drama, you should know:

- Why your idea is suited for an audio drama medium.
- What goals and milestones you want to reach.
- How much time and money you can dedicate to production.

- What your strengths are (in equipment and expertise).
- What your weaknesses are (in equipment and expertise).
- How long or short your episodes and first season will be.

Every show starts with an idea. Maybe it's "I would want to listen to this!" or "Wouldn't it be cool if?", perhaps a "I bet people would be into that . . ." or "Why is nobody doing this?" Your idea doesn't have to be a fully fleshed out concept at the start. In fact, it might be better if you start with something flexible, because you'll need to modify it down the road as you learn what that idea needs to do. Modifying your idea to better work as an audio drama is a common part of production.

You don't need to come at this with a detailed outline. A simple concept will do. Your idea could be a general plot, some characters, and/or a few emotional beats. It's a sandbox to play in. And we're going to *play*.

Some simple concept examples:

- Town that is Weird (*Welcome to Night Vale*)
- Wizard dating show (*Wizard Seeking Wizard*)
- Two people leave each other voicemails (*Love & Luck*)
- Therapy for teens with superpowers (*The Bright Sessions*)

- Person alone in Antarctica (*Station Blue*)
- Six girls inadvertently summon a demon (*Calling Darkness*)
- Adventurer avoids the main plot (*Sidequesting*)
- It's literally Dracula (*Re: Dracula*)

The concept of your show will define your brand identity, determine how easy or hard it is for your podcast to produce, control your budget, and make or break your listenership. The heart of any audio drama is what it's about, and you're stuck with it once you get going.

For example, I couldn't pivot *Sidequesting* into a gothic horror down the road, because the concept of the show revolves around it being lighthearted fantasy. It's never going to have giant robot fights or street races, there's never going to be an intense breakup between two characters or emotional, heart-wrenching monologues. If I wanted any of this in my production, I would have had to change the concept from the start.

Here's another example. *What Will Be Here* is about a group of friends building their version of the Voyager Record on a planet doomed from late-stage capitalism and climate change. It touches on some dark topics — grief, fascism, plague . . . it was written during lockdown in 2020, if that gives you an idea. I poured a lot of my fear and bitterness into this show, and I knew from the beginning it wasn't getting a very happy ending.

Within this concept, moments of levity had to be earned (unlike *Sidequesting*, where moments of levity make up the entire show). The audience was set up for tension from the beginning. Pivoting *What Will Be Here* into something cute and sweet was not in the cards because of the premise of the show. It's in the "apocalyptic sci-fi" genre for a reason.

Within your story idea, think about what you and your audience would want to hear — and I mean that literally. Decide why *sound* is the sensory input you want for your audience. What elements of sound are going to elevate your story? Why isn't it a film, a game, or a novel? What about it works for audio? We'll cover this in more depth later on, but for now, just keep it in mind.

What Will Be Here works for audio because it's audio found footage. The Voyager Record included visuals, but the biggest part of it was a global audio recording, and I wanted to mimic that. The story revolves around the audio that is being recorded in-universe.

Sidequesting works for audio because it's about mundane things. It would also have worked as a book or comic, but I liked the intimacy of having first-person narration right into the audience's ears. I also enjoyed elevating the story with music and sound design. In *Sidequesting*, I wanted the audience to get the sensory input of walking in a forest or visiting a medieval town. Basically, I wanted listeners to feel like they're along for a side quest.

In this way, you don't need your idea to be about a recording for it to work in audio. You just need your idea to use the medium of audio to its advantage by creating scenes that work well without a visual element.

Defining the Scope

The key to a good audio drama idea lies in its use of the medium. A story like *Interstellar*, with its famous CGI shots of black holes and wide camera pans across stunning planets? Remove the visuals and it's kind of boring. An action scene from *The Matrix* would be difficult to follow from sound alone. What would a fantasy TV show be without the costuming? Can you keep track of a long-running drama without faces to keep the characters straight?

Knowing what works in audio is key to making something in audio, so we've got to start there. The most important thing to remember is that there are no visuals.

Imagine this, heard by a listener: *The sound of a chair scraping, followed by another. Echoing footfalls. The sound of something crashing, then several thumps. "Get them!" is shouted by the voice actor playing Doctor Basil. The sound of feet pattering answers. Another thump.*

Imagine this, read by a narrator: "Rose leaps out of her chair, sprinting to the door. Lily follows, pulling the contents of a bookshelf down to block the path." (*"Get them!" is shouted by the voice actor playing Doctor Basil.)* "Lab assistants scramble after them. One slips on the books and falls."

This scene would have to be set up very carefully for a listener to know the context of this budding chase from the sounds alone, without a narrator. Presumably, before a scene starts, some information would be obvious. The audience would know Rose and Lily are with Doctor Basil in a room, probably some sort of lab where other technicians are present. There might be some sort of tense discussion (a threat by the doctor, perhaps?) that justifies a swift exit by the duo and chase by the doctor's team. But at this moment, how is a listener to know that Rose goes first and Lily follows? That it was a bookshelf that got pulled down, and that one of the lab assistants slipped on a book? Which direction are they running in?

Some questions a sound designer might have, even with the context provided by the narration, include: How many lab assistants are there? Are they big and burly or small and slight? How large is this room? How far do Rose and Lily have to run to not get caught? What is the floor made of? Are Lily and Rose wearing tennis shoes or something more formal? Who is wearing clothes that might rustle? They might decide the answers to some of these on their own, or discuss with the showrunner. This information is not necessary for a listener to know, but it's necessary to create the sounds that build this scene.

The sound designer's files might look something like: chair_scrape1, chair_scrape2, jacket_rustle1, shoe_scrape1, sportshoe_running_tile_1, sportshoe_running_tile_2, (*A reverb plugin to manage the echo*), shoe_scrape2, wood_creak1, wood_crash1, wood_spliter1, book_drop1, book_drop2, book_drop3 (*and so on*), (*there are probably a lot of books falling*), smartshoe_running_tile_1, smartshoe_running_tile_2, smartshoe_running_tile_3, book_slide1, shoe_slide1, bodyfall_medium_tile_hands1, bodyfall_medium_knees1, and jacket_rustle2.

A sound designer may also request that the actors playing Lily and Rose provide some heavy breathing to layer under the running scene. It could be beneficial to have a grunt from

Lily for when the bookcase is pulled down, and a cry from the lab assistant when they fall. These would be layered in with the other files.

From my own experience as a sound designer, I know this short scene would be tricky to pull off. It requires a significant investment in time to find these sound effects (also called SFX), get incidental audio from actors, and layer everything with the right timing. Even after all that work, the events of the scene may not be fully clear without narration due to the no-visuals format of the audio drama medium.

It's also likely that this isn't a one-off occurrence for the show. If you have two protagonists getting into trouble and an antagonist with minions to direct after them, you're almost certainly writing in other action-packed scenes. Each scene requires all this work, all over again. If you can't budget for a professional sound designer, and especially if you're a one-person team, this is going to delay and complicate production.

This is what I mean when I say your idea needs to work with audio. If you already have an idea for an audio drama, think about what parts of that idea rely on sight, and how you can utilize dialogue and sound effects instead.

To Narrate or Not to Narrate

If your audio drama concept depends on visuals, you'd best incorporate a narrator. Sound design can get many things across (such as the sound of a punch), but is limited in other areas (such as making it clear who punched who). There are all sorts of techniques you can use to make action and setting clear without narration, but having a narrator is the simplest and cheapest option, and therefore a great place for first time shows to start.

A narrator is a cost-saving measure if you're paying for sound design, and a time-saving measure if you're doing sound design on your own. If this audio drama will be your first time trying out sound design, utilizing a narrator for complex sequences can save you from writing yourself into a corner.

For example, *Sidequesting* is a show that features a first-person narrator. The main character, Rion, jumps in with narration between scenes and occasionally within them.

I've utilized narration when:

- The characters are traveling between places and I want to jump from one spot to another
- I want a time cut between scenes that take place in the same location (like going to bed and waking up the next day)
- Our main character meets someone new and describes them to the listener
- Action packed scenes occur that I don't want to sound design

For this last category, I know while I'm writing episodes of *Sidequesting* that I will be the one sound designing them. I know what sound effects I have in my library, what plugins I have (plugins are software that can be used to modify and enhance audio — think vocal effects), and generally what I can and cannot do. I also know what sorts of action will take a long time to sound design. Sometimes I want to take the time to get really deep into a scene. Other times I want to focus my efforts elsewhere in a story. I don't have infinite time to produce an episode, so I have to choose what I want to dedicate my hours to. Making parts of the production process faster and more efficient means I can spend more time on other parts.

When I want something to happen in an episode of *Sidequesting* that I either can't or don't want to sound design, I have it happen during narration. Having a narrator gives me this flexibility. Without it, I would have to write only what I was willing to sound design, which would limit the stories I could tell.

But it's not all or nothing! A narrator can also be a great way to dip your toes into sound design by layering some of these sounds under the narration. Going back to the scene above, I'd pick the footsteps, a crash for the bookshelf, and a bodyfall sound for the lab assistant falling. Instead of carrying the action, this underlying sound works to *elevate* the narration. I utilized this style of sound design in *Re: Dracula*, picking key moments with interesting and significant sounds to play under the narration. It keeps listeners engaged and prevents confusion.

Though, maybe you don't want a narrator. In this case, you should make sure your idea works without one. This doesn't have to mean learning complicated sound design from scratch — it could mean having an idea that doesn't require complicated sound design. This can be as simple as not having complicated action scenes, or having those scenes occur "offscreen."

My favorite example of this is *Inn Between*, which follows a band of fantasy adventurers between their adventures. The fighting happens mostly between episodes, and listeners get to hear the debrief between the fights, which happens at an inn. It's a very clever concept!

Ultimately, it'll be easier to make your concept work for your production instead of the other way around. Know how you want your piece to sound before you lock down the concept, so that you can change your story idea before you're stuck. This could mean changing the genre, removing a few characters, adding a narrator, removing some episodes, or adding a framing device.

Playing with Genre

Sometimes complicated sound design is limited by genre. *The Bright Sessions,* a slice of life/urban sci-fi, features a first season made almost exclusively out of recorded therapy sessions. People sit and talk, and connections (and a plot) are slowly revealed through these meetings. There were usually no more than two people in a room, they rarely moved around, and they mostly just talked. Intense sound design would have been out of place. But the conversions were fascinating!

However, sound design can also be *complicated* by genre. If you don't have sound design experience in another field, you probably shouldn't do an action-based space opera for your first show. This genre relies heavily on sound effects and requires a large amount of sound design. Your choice of genre could determine what you need to prepare for. For example, if you're making a musical audio drama, you'll need skills you otherwise could go without.

Your genre will guide your audience's expectations, which means it controls, in part, what a listener expects from your show. If having listeners is important to you, then you have to cater to their expectations on some level so that they stick with your production.

Slice of Life media can be down to earth and simple. You can also combine Slice of Life with other genres too (like fantasy, in the case of my show *Sidequesting*). A mystery show needs a mystery and people to solve it, but it can take place anywhere, even in a single room. Horror shows can have a very simple setup, as long as there is something scary. In genres like this, the audience isn't expecting something big and grand. It doesn't mean you're limited to a small and unimpressive set, but rather that the audience won't be disappointed to see (or in our case, *hear*) a set like this.

Meanwhile, if you're attempting something in the action/thriller department, there better be action and it better be thrilling. An Epic Fantasy needs to be fantasy that is epic. If the genre of your story demands large set pieces and sweeping orchestral music and dramatic monologues — you need to be prepared to do them.

Let's put it this way: How would you feel if you sat down for a *James Bond* movie and Daniel Craig walked around a house trying to solve a murder? Probably like you made popcorn for nothing. If *Knives Out* had a scene where Daniel Craig climbed the side of a high-rise, you'd probably wonder if you put the wrong movie on.

The genre of your audio drama doesn't decide what you have to do, but it decides what a listener expects to happen.

Meet (or subvert) those expectations, or face disappointment.

Have the Skills and Tools for Your Idea

Sometimes to make a good show you must kill your darlings, and sometimes those darlings are ambitious action scenes. Because you don't need action scenes to have a good audio drama. In fact, having confusing, poorly sound designed action scenes is often worse than having none at all.

If your idea is too ambitious, you should scale back, or your audio drama is going to fall short. "Too ambitious" means the skills you presently have on hand cannot meet the concept in your head. Sound effects or music may not be quite right, scenes may be confusing or boring, and most crucially, your audience will be disappointed and stop listening to your work.

Defining the scope of your audio drama means more than just working out how you're managing the visuals. It also means working with what you have on hand. The tools to bring your idea to life should be accessible for you *right now*. This goes beyond action scenes vs. no action scenes.

For example, if you don't have a good microphone or the funds to get one (and you're planning on using that mic in the podcast), consider setting up your show so that it works with less-than-great audio. You could use a framing device: perhaps a character is recording in-universe, and they don't have access to a great mic. Or maybe this is an old recording on a cassette tape that's just been unearthed. Perhaps it's a transmission from an alien planet.

Some examples of audio dramas with a framing device are:

- *Welcome to Night Vale*
- *Stories from Ylelmore*
- *Podcube*
- *Shelterwood*
- *The Black Tapes*
- *The Bright Sessions*
- *Less is Morgue*

Maybe the characters are communicating over the phone or radio, where some level of distortion makes sense. This format can be found in *Love and Luck, ROGUEMAKER,* and *World Gone Wrong*. Perhaps the character using this mic is a robot or AI, and there will be effects over the voice that make pristine audio quality unnecessary.

Some examples of audio dramas with Robot or AI characters include:

- *Dining in the Void*
- *Wolf 359*
- *Startripper!!*
- *Girl in Space*
- *What Will Be Here?*

A listener who is provided an excuse for "bad" audio is more likely to stick with a show that has it, because in this case, it's an intentional part of the show and not a detriment to the production quality.

Avoid Complications

As with my suggestion to avoid complicated sound design if you're new to sound designing, you should avoid complications in other aspects of production if you're new to them as well. The central idea here is that you can and should modify your idea to play to what you're good at.

I want you to keep the scope of your show in mind as you learn more about the intricacies of production, and be willing to head back to the drawing board to refine your idea as necessary. This is why it's beneficial to keep the concept of your show flexible. As you learn what does and doesn't work, you can modify that concept to lean into what *does* work.

For example, if you're planning to play a character, and you're new to acting, consider avoiding heavily emotional scenes until you're sure you can nail them. (But someone coming to audio drama production from acting might create a character for themself to play that has many juicy scenes). If you're new to managing a bunch of schedules, consider planning on asynchronous recording — having your actors record their lines on their own time and sending you their audio files — instead of live sessions with remote voice actors across different time zones. Or work with local friends that are easy to get a hold of! If you're not a strong writer, avoid a script that hinges on intricately revealed twists and complicated plot beats.

If you're planning to do all the voices in your show, limit the number of characters to the distinct voices you can produce (Examples of one-person productions include: *InCo*, *Desert Skies*, and *Malevolent*). If you're planning on working with voice actors, consider keeping the number of characters lower anyway so that you're managing fewer people to begin with. Every character you add means a new voice actor to onboard, new schedules to work with, and one more thing to keep track of. Each character adds complexity and introduces potential complications.

Combining characters in the writing phase or having voice actors voice multiple minor or one-off characters in the production phase, is a way to manage the scope of your audio drama. Keep in mind that every character you add is another person the audience has to keep track of, too.

It's similar to what I said about confusing action scenes: having an emotional scene that falls flat is often worse than not having it at all. Same for a confusing plot twist. Or unnecessary extra characters. The list goes on. Allow yourself to pare down your audio drama script until only the best parts remain. If that means less episodes and fewer characters, so be it! You're making your show better.

Decreasing episode and season length is a great way to decrease the scope of your production. It's possible your favorite show does half hour episodes, and you want to do that too because it's what you're used to. However, if you decide to do 15-minute episodes instead, production will take half as long. Starting with a ten episode season instead of planning 30 episodes will make your show three times as doable. In general, having long episode lengths for the sake of having a long episode lengths often leads to burnout and forced writing to fill the minutes.

There is no standard expectation for episode length in audio drama. Some shows have two- or five-minute episodes, some have ten or 15, others go 30 to 45, and a few surpass an hour. Think about what works best for the format of your script and the process of your production.

If the scripts you write wrap up nicely in about 20 minutes, that's great. If you feel pulled towards microfiction and shorter episodes, go in that direction. In general, it's a good idea to have consistent episode lengths across a season, but if you create the expectation of wildly different episode lengths for your show from the beginning, listeners will be okay with it.

Examples of the above:

- Two- to five-minute episodes: *InCo*, *Falling Forward*, some episodes of *Re: Dracula*
- Ten- to 15-minute episodes: *Sidequesting*, *Someone Dies In This Elevator, Inn Between, The Goblet Wire, Absolutely No Adventures*
- 30- to 45-minute episodes: *Tales of the Echowood, VALENCE, The Holmwood Foundation, Starship Q Star, The Harbingers*
- 1-hour (or longer) episodes: Some episodes of *Re: Dracula, Edict Zero FIS*

Remember that you get to decide how easy or hard production is. I'm giving you permission to make it easier on yourself — it's more likely you'll meet your goals if you do! It can be disappointing having to decrease the scope of your audio drama, to kill darlings and shelf ideas. But when you find yourself doing this, keep in mind that you're making your production better for it. Every single thing you remove can always be used for a different idea or show later.

I bring this all up early on because it's easiest to define your scope in the ideation stage. You can shift genres, combine characters, add a narrator, change action scenes, and more, all without extensive rewrites. When you think about how you're going to bring your audio drama idea to life before you make it happen, you can foresee difficulties and plan for them ahead of time, or avoid them entirely. Look at the technical tools and skills you have available (and more important, those you don't have), and create a concept that can accommodate these limitations. If you do this, you won't find yourself hitting your head against a wall in post-production to make a scene you wrote work.

Chapter 3

The Job of a Showrunner

Job titles in audio drama are all over the place. What's a showrunner, and how is it different from a producer? Ask and you'll get a bunch of different answers. However, the responsibilities of a showrunner are important and worth understanding, even if people use different terms for them.

For this book, I'll be using the terms "showrunner" and "producer" interchangeably. The showrunner is the person in charge of the audio drama. They're running the show. It doesn't get made without them. They are producing it. I'm assuming that you, the aspiring creator of an audio drama, will be the showrunner and producer.

The indie audio drama producer wears many hats. Production teams are often small, and the person who wants the show to happen most must fill in all the extra roles needed for it.

As showrunner, you might find yourself doing any number of these jobs:

Pre-Production:

- Writer

- Script Editor
- Casting Director

Production:

- Voice Actor
- Vocal Director
- Human Resources
- Project Manager
- Recording Engineer

Post-Production:

- Dialogue Editor
- Sound Designer
- Composer
- Transcriber
- Graphic Designer
- Social Media Manager
- Publicity Director
- Crowdfunding Manager

If any of these roles are unfamiliar, here's a quick breakdown:

Pre-Production:

The writer writes the script, and the script editor edits it. A graphic designer creates visual assets for the show, including cover art and social media graphics. The casting director oversees auditioning and casting voice actors.

Production:

Voice actors perform the voices of the audio drama. Actors may be directed by a vocal director.

Post Production:

The dialogue editor takes the raw recordings and cuts it to match the script. The sound designer adds sound effects on top of that. The composer creates music for the show. The transcriber takes the script and finished audio and creates a transcript.

All Stages of Production:

The social media manager handles the social media for the audio drama. The project manager oversees the scheduling and progress of production, including recording sessions and post-production deadlines. The publicity manager oversees the marketing and promotion strategy for the show, often working closely with the social media and project managers. Human resources ensure there are no interpersonal issues among the cast and crew.

The most common jobs I see outsourced are: composers, voice actors, sound designers, dialogue editors, transcribers, and graphic designers (this list is roughly ordered from most common to least common). Showrunners are most often doing their own writing, and frequently doing their own directing, script editing, and graphic design. Showrunners tend to voice one character in their production and hire additional voice actors, or voice no one at all, and, least frequently, voice everyone. Outside of casting, I see occasional calls for musicians, audio editors, and people to create transcripts.

But almost every indie producer does their own casting, manages their own social media, oversees the production schedule, handles marketing and publicity, and is their own HR department. If a show is crowdfunding, the showrunner is overseeing the campaign.

This can be a bunch of un-fun work for something that's supposed to be a hobby — work that you potentially don't have training on. And beyond that, these jobs are rarely talked about publicly or credited to the producer anywhere. In indie audio drama, it's all assumed to be done under the title of "showrunner."

Because these jobs aren't openly discussed, they can come as a surprise to new showrunners. Few people make an audio drama with the hopes of teaching themselves social media marketing or project management. Typically, they're in it for the creative parts.

But the strategic parts are vital to a successful audio drama. You might find joy in them, or satisfaction solely in checking them off a list. But the more time and effort you dedicate to the administrative parts like scheduling, the smoother your audio drama will run.

There's no easy way to learn how to do any of this, but I hope by reading this book you'll get an idea of how to start and what to do next. In my experience, the best way to learn is by doing. No matter how prepared you are, there are going to be surprises. Get ready to roll with the punches, but don't be afraid to jump in head first.

The Human Resources Discussion

As showrunner, you're also the HR manager for your production. If you're running a solo production, or working with a few friends, this probably isn't a big job. But as soon as you start bringing on additional cast and crew, it becomes one. This section is geared towards creators in the latter situation, though laying out expectations clearly among friends wouldn't hurt.

Being HR means that if disputes break out in your team, you'll have to manage the situation. If these disputes involve you personally, things will get messy quickly. The best way to handle issues like this is to create a clear set of expectations and guidelines, and outline how disputes will be handled before they happen. One way to do this is to create a code of conduct for cast and crew. This can be a short document that outlines the boundaries of your team and what will happen when those boundaries are crossed.

Here is an example code of conduct for voice actors I used in one of my shows:

If an actor engages in behavior that creates an unsafe work environment for any of the cast/crew during their time working for the show, they will be removed from their role in the show. The actor will receive notice from the showrunner via email of their removal and reason for it. Such behavior includes:

- *Making inappropriate or insulting remarks.*

- *Asking inappropriate questions about a person's race, gender, gender identity, religion, color, national origin, ancestry, sexual orientation, or ability.*
- *Asking persistent, unwanted questions about someone's private life.*
- *Demanding favors from cast and crew (especially with a promise of rewards for complying or punishment for refusal).*

Outside of working on the show, if an actor is found to have engaged in hate speech, bullying, abuse, or sexual harassment, they will be removed from their role in the show.

If the showrunner is made aware of such actions after the actor has been cast but before lines have been received, the actor will be recast without payment. Prompt notice will be given to the actor via email so that unpaid work is not done.

If the showrunner is made aware of such actions after lines have been recorded but before the episode has been released, the actor will be recast, but will keep their payment for work rendered. Notice will be given to the actor via email.

If the showrunner is made aware of such actions after the episode featuring the actor has been released, the show may make a public statement on social media so that such actions are not endorsed by the show. In some extreme cases, the episode may be re-released with a different actor (in this case, notice will be given to the actor via email). The showrunner will make the decision as to what type of response is warranted.

You may copy from and modify this code of conduct for your own production if desired. It was made for an anthology-style show where actors were only in one episode at a time. Recasting before episode release was therefore a simpler prospect than with a recurring character. If your situation is different, you might need to adjust this code of conduct for what will work for you.

Dealing with Minor Conflict

The code of conduct is meant to cover behavior that creates an unsafe workplace — in other words, egregious behavior. You may not need a strict code of conduct for creative disagreements or minor conflicts, but it may be helpful to informally lay out how you plan to deal with those. As showrunner, it's on you to prevent passive-aggressive and rude behavior. It's possible you'll have to tell someone kindly but firmly to knock something off.

In short, making it clear how you plan to respond to negative behavior provides a distinct path of action during a stressful situation. If you already have a tense relationship with a team member, a pre-signed code of conduct will make it clear you're not targeting them. Establishing expectations from the get-go will also decrease the chances of someone accidentally crossing a line.

It will also be useful to outline who on the crew has decision-making authority, especially if your audio drama has multiple producers. If creative differences occur between producers, both may push to get their way. Determining how decisions will be made before any decisions need to be made will prevent tension. It's okay to say, "As showrunner, I will make all final decisions," but if you are co-running a production, that's probably not fair.

Have Multiple Pathways for Reporting

It's beneficial for a team to have multiple paths of reporting. Consider employing an artist's representative that the cast and crew can speak with if they have issues with you. This creates a check on your power as showrunner and allows individuals who are intimidated by the person in charge to go to an advocate specifically there for them. Having an artist's representative will decrease the likelihood of a smaller problem going unreported and festering into a larger one. It will also decrease the likelihood of a cast or crew member feeling uncomfortable about something and helpless to address it.

This artist's representative could be a cast or crew member, or someone with no other roles in the production. They will act as an intermediary between the cast/crew and the showrunner. This means that if the showrunner does something harmful to a cast member, that person does not have to report to the person who harmed them. The person you hire as an artist's representative should be someone you trust, someone that is willing to have hard conversations, and someone that will call you in when you cross a boundary.

Put Your Best Foot Forward

The power dynamic between the showrunner and the rest of their team cannot be ignored, even if everyone is a volunteer, even if everyone is close friends. The showrunner holds power over everyone else and therefore is in a position to abuse that power. The showrunner can set deadlines, make demands of cast and crew members' time, determine how cast and crew are promoted on social media, manage the show budget and payments, and create the culture behind production.

Any one of these things can be done in a harmful way, both maliciously and completely unintentionally. Because of this, it is imperative to build safety guidelines into your show. If a situation arises where a cast or crew member feels mistreated by you, there should be a pre-established pathway for that person to safely report this.

Even if you're making audio drama as a fun hobby, it's important to remember that not everyone who joins your project is there to be your friend. If an actor you bring onto the project just wants to send you lines and be done, let them. Don't pressure cast and crew to engage with you or your show beyond their established job. For example, cast and crew game nights or episode listening parties should not be mandatory. If you didn't establish it up front, you shouldn't require social media posts or other promotion from your cast and crew (I recommend not requiring it at all).

It seems obvious that once you bring people beyond your close friends into your passion project, you need to act professionally and treat them professionally. But these lines are easily blurred, especially when those close friends are still part of the project. It's your job as showrunner to keep in mind the changing scene of your production if and when you grow. Establish a production schedule and stick with it, clearly communicate deadlines, and avoid discussion of personal topics.

It's also your job as showrunner to mind the power differential in your production. I don't mean only as boss/employees; when you're working with members of marginalized groups, you need to ensure your show is a safe environment for them. White people: learn about the different experiences of people of color. Cisgender people: learn about the trans experience. Abled people: learn about the disabled experience. And so on, and so forth.

An essential part of ensuring your show is a safe environment is implementing a zero-tolerance policy for microaggressions. These are indirect, subtle, and/or unintentional discrimination against members of a marginalized group. Not tolerating microaggressions in your production requires that you can identify and respond to these behaviors when they occur. If you are unfamiliar with common microaggressions people working with you face, it's your responsibility to learn more about them and develop a strategy to intervene. Prepare to learn and grow, and you'll have a better show as a result.

Chapter 4

Write for Sound

You should have a general sense for why your audio drama idea is suited for the medium from the earlier "Defining Your Scope" section, and now it's time to dive in deeper. How do you make *every scene* in your audio drama suited for the medium? You write for sound.

Writing for sound is not only about complicated action sequences; it's about the small stuff too. Each action a character takes needs to be understood by a listener.

A character taking a drink of water might sound like: chair creak (if they're sitting down) + picking up a cup + a sipping noise + putting a cup down.

A character picking up their bag and leaving a room might sound like: clothes rustle + bag rustle + footsteps + door close.

A character preparing a dinner might sound like: kitchen drawer open + silverware clatter + knife set on table + cabinet open + wooden cutting board sliding out + wooden cutting board thump on kitchen counter + plastic packing rustle + potato thump on cutting board + cutting sounds.

Deceptively simple notes, like "doing the dishes" or "setting the table" can become very complicated, very quickly. I recommend thinking about how a sound note might be broken down into smaller pieces, and including those smaller pieces in the notes.

For example, instead of writing "Helen leaves the room," you might add "footsteps followed by a door opening and closing." You can get as granular as you want: "high-heeled footsteps on wood, metal door opens and closes, now-muffled footsteps fade out." The former is good enough if you're hiring a sound designer (they'll likely decide the shoes, floor type, and door material), but if you're doing your own sound design, detailed notes from "writer-you" will help "sound designer–you".

But not everything can be explained with sound. Here are some sound effect (SFX) notes that will make your sound designer cry:

- "The room is dark and rounded."
- "He is wearing a red t-shirt and jeans."
- "There is a large painting on the wall."
- "They frown and shake their head."
- "The mysterious man waves."
- "She picks up a pair of jeans."

What do any of these sound like? Or rather, is there a sound that a listener can hear and know it is exactly that thing? No! Writing sound notes is different from writing stage directions; you need a specific *sound* in mind when you describe what's present or what happens. Simply stating what that thing is (or what it looks like) isn't enough. And if that specific sound you have in mind is the only piece of information for a listener to know what's present or what's happening, it needs to be distinct.

Expecting a listener to know the type of material a fabric is made out of based on the sound of it is not feasible. Neither is expecting them to identify a specific car based on the sound. In the right context, silverware sounds are identifiable, and something ceramic in the same setting would usually be assumed to be a plate or cup. A listener can probably identify the sound of a gun loading, but a crossbow or longbow? Less likely.

You can always determine if a sound is identifiable by getting a friend to listen to it without knowing what it is. But if nobody is available, you'd best err on the side of caution.

Not all notes are crucial for an audience. You might write "they frown and lean back" as a performance note for an actor. It's not important that a listener understands the specific actions, but rather that the voice actor understands and doesn't give a cheerful performance. But if a character frowning and leaning back is a crucial part of plot development, you'd best have another character comment on it in the dialogue. It's the same for set dressing (a painting on the wall), outfits (a character wearing a red shirt), and silent actions (shaking hands). If a note is visual and important, say it out loud. Ultimately, sound design should enhance dialogue, not replace it.

Let's explore a note like "Anna picks up a mirror and looks into it." You might have a sound for "metallic object is picked up," potentially with some sort of "*shing*" layered in — but how will a listener know it's a mirror and not a knife? You'll have to make it clear within the dialogue.

For example:

```
Helen: You're blushing.
Anna: I'm not blushing. Am I blushing?
[SFX: Anna picks up a mirror and looks into it.]
Anna: Oh my god I'm blushing.
Helen: The mirror doesn't lie.
```

The exchange before the sound note builds context. Anna's first response to Helen indicates that she wants to see if her face is indeed red. This gives a listener a clue that Anna is the one picking up the mirror, not Helen. It gives a second clue for the listener to narrow down the objects that might have been picked up. Technically, a glass or a knife could give Anna her reflection, but a mirror makes the most sense. Helen's response at the end confirms the object.

If a listener imagined the wrong thing being picked up, they're only incorrect for a line. The "and looks into it" part of the note becomes a short pause in the dialogue, but it's generally understood that the thing you do with a mirror is look at it, so a listener knows what the pause means.

Writing for sound requires a balance between dialogue and sound notes, all in the name of listener clarity.

Here's a worse version of that exchange:

```
Helen: You're blushing.
[SFX: Anna picks up a mirror and looks into it.]
Anna: Oh my god I'm blushing.
```

Who picked up the object? What *was* the object? A listener can probably piece it together (something was grabbed and now Anna knows what her face looks like . . . a mirror!) but if a single piece of the puzzle is missed, the scene becomes unclear and the listener becomes confused. For something like this, you need the dialogue to come in and balance the sound note. Without additional dialogue, the note isn't clear. Unclear sound notes will add to listener confusion, especially if they think the sound is clear, but they imagine something entirely different.

If the sound you include doesn't evoke an image in the ballpark of what you want, that's a problem. But something like:

```
Helen: You're blushing.
[SFX: a metal object is picked up]
Anna: Oh my god I'm blushing.
```

or:

```
Helen: You're blushing.
[SFX: a beat of silence]
Anna: Oh my god I'm blushing.
```

Could work if a listener not realizing a mirror is present won't break your story. Maybe it's not an important part of the scene. Perhaps this is a comedic exchange meant to display Helen and Anna's relationship, and the mirror isn't mentioned again. You might have set the scene in a bedroom or living room, a place where one might have a mirror or compact within reach. The conversation works on dialogue alone. In this scenario, the sound is not load bearing, so it's okay if it's unclear *as long as* it doesn't lead your listener astray. Big BIG emphasis on "as long as"!

Doing this is inherently a risky thing. A listener could be so caught up thinking "what was that supposed to be?" or "what happened there? Did I miss something?" that they stop following the scene and miss something actually important. I recommend using dialogue to make actions clear in order to avoid these aforementioned scenarios. Save your potentially unclear sound effects to enhance the environmental ambiance — or do yourself a favor and make everything clear.

For building an environment, sound design can be used both to enhance a scene *and* as a crucial part of the story. Enhancing a scene takes the existing vibes of a setting and turns it up a notch. A scary scene gets scarier with startling creaks and foreboding drones. A cozy scene gets cozier with sounds of a warm fireplace and cat purring. A sci-fi ship can be enhanced with bleeps and bloops. A fantasy forest can be enhanced with bird calls and a bubbling brook. You can create these scenes without the specific sound effects I've mentioned and still maintain an atmosphere, but adding these sounds makes it *better*.

For example, a fantasy forest with rustling leaves from a breeze and crunchy sticks underfoot will still read as a fantasy forest without the bird calls or bubbling brook. A sci-fi ship with fewer bleeps and bloops will still read as a sci-fi ship if you've got the automatic sliding doors, footsteps on metal, and the drone of engines in the background. You don't need a roaring fireplace or a purring cat in order to have a cozy scene — but you need *something*. When it comes to building an environment, the base SFX that establish the environment are crucial. But once you've got a collection of sounds that sell where your characters are, you can always enhance it by adding more details.

If a sound note is unclear, but that sound is merely enhancement, it doesn't affect clarity. If you can remove the sound note and maintain understanding (of the scene's environment or the actions taking place), it's not a load bearing sound. If removing a sound makes the scene become confusing and unclear, that sound is a crucial part of the story.

A good learning experience might be to take one of your scripts and highlight SFX notes that are load bearing. Once you've done this, go back and make sure each note is clear and non-visual.

Script writing for audio drama is not screenwriting. First-time writers (especially those coming from a screen or playwright background) can struggle with this. It can be tempting to write camera cuts and close up shots into your script, but remember, these mean nothing in an audio-only medium. There is no one-to-one replacement for them, either.

Writing for audio requires a shift in thinking to describe a setting with sound alone. Here are some examples of how to set a scene with sounds:

- A spooky castle: low drone, mysterious creaking, large echoes, footsteps on tile
- A bedroom: muffled sound of a nearby road, hum of fan, ticking of a clock
- A restaurant: silverware clinking, overlapping conversations, distant sounds of a kitchen
- A city sidewalk: cars passing, distant construction sounds, people walking, ambient chit chat
- A beach: waves crashing, seagulls squawking, footsteps on sand

The key is pulling a collection of sounds that elicit the visuals you want. This can usually be left to the sound designer (you can say "EXT: crowded beach" and they'll know what to do with that), but you don't have to make them guess. A sound designer will be happy to read "EXT: a crowded beach. There are crashing waves and lots of seagull noises. The beach is full of families on vacation; kids shout happily as they play."

They will be less happy to read "EXT: A crowded beach. It's a hot day, there are colorful umbrellas as far as the eye can see. Lifeguards supervise the kids in the ocean while the parents play with children on the sand." The first note gives an idea of how you want the scene to sound, but the second note gives an idea of how you want the scene to look. The sound designer *can* work with this, but nobody is going to hear the color of the umbrellas or the presence of lifeguard towers. They'll hear the waves of the ocean and the shouts of kids playing in it. (Are those umbrellas or lifeguards important to your scene? Have a character comment on it!)

Writing sound notes for the action and sound notes for the environment boil down to the same thing. If it's important, make sure it's clear.

For example, if you're writing a scene in a forest, and you want the audience to know there is a specific type of bird there, only including that bird's call will not be enough. Listeners will know there is a bird, but only the most dedicated of birdwatchers in your fan base will identify the type. If there's a stream in the forest, and you want the audience to know it's a very dangerous fast moving stream, only having the sound of a fast moving stream will not be enough. Listeners will know there is a stream, but only the white water rafting instructors in your fan base will know it's a dangerous one.

Writing for sound means knowing the limits of sound, and occasionally moving key information to dialogue or narration. It's also about keeping the constraints of the medium in your mind while you write your script. You can't depend on visuals to carry a scene, nor can you depend on sound effects to get the same amount of information across as an image might.

Narrators in Sound Design

Having a narrator certainly makes writing for sound easier. Instead of worrying if the dialogue and sound effects are working together for clarity, you can simply have your narrator say what's important.

However, if you're using a narrator *and* sound effects, timing becomes complicated. It can be faster OR slower to talk about someone doing something than it is to do it. If your narrator is describing an action scene, and you plan on having sounds for every part of that action scene underneath, the timing isn't going to sound correct. A good middle ground is to pick and choose which sounds you want to have instead of using all of them. But even with this tactic, you have to accept that SFX and narration will not always line up.

"Jerry runs down the hallway and unlocks the door" is a sentence that is faster to say than to do. If you're dedicated to having footsteps for the entire length of the hallway, you're going to have to pause the narrator for the sound to catch up. A good compromise might be to have running sounds under "Jerry runs down the hallway" and accept that the length of running is less than if there was no narration.

"Jerry quickly turns the knob and peeks into a small apartment. Determining that the coast is clear, he rushes in, slamming the door behind him. He double-checks the main lock and engages the secondary bolt on the door," is a narration that is faster to do than to say. If you include the sounds for turning the knob, entering the room, slamming the door, checking a lock, and engaging a second lock, you're going to have pauses between sounds where the narrator must catch up. If you're dedicated to having the timing of the SFX correct, the listener will hear that second lock turning while the narrator is talking about Jerry rushing in. Modifying the timing of the SFX is the good compromise here.

Some people shy away from a narrator, worried it's too audiobook-like or some sort of cop out. I'm here to tell you that neither are true. Having a narrator can be great, and you can get weird and have fun with it. Unreliable narrators, narrators who are characters but you don't quite know how they fit in yet, narrators who are the main characters . . . you've got options. Naturally, narrators don't work in every type of show, and if you're struggling to include one, it's okay to swing the other way too!

For example, *What Will Be Here* didn't work with a third-person narrator due to the framing device utilized throughout the whole show. The characters would narrate their thoughts to an audio recorder, and there were a few action scenes where the recorder was accidentally turned on. Having a narrator during these action scenes would have been scene-breakingly out of place (Who is talking to the audience? Why are they doing that?). In contrast, for scenes where a character intentionally turned a recorder on and started talking into it, first-person narration felt natural.

Other Writing Advice

There are a few things to keep in mind beyond simply writing for sound.

Keep Character Count Low(ish)

You can get away with having more characters in a novel than you can with audio drama. Every character you add not only increases your workload in regard to casting and scheduling voice actors, but it's another voice for listeners to keep track of.

Group scenes are difficult to write because characters need to speak for the audience to know their feelings, and it becomes a balancing act to manage three or more characters in a scene. This is because the more characters there are in a scene, the more time characters will spend listening to others talk (and therefore, saying nothing themselves). Think about mingling in a large group at a party. Chances are, only a few people are regularly speaking. In a visual medium, you can see all the people in this group and keep them in mind. In an audio medium, this isn't possible. You've got to hear someone speak to remember they're there.

Don't be afraid to combine characters in the idea stage or early writing process. If you must have a large cast, have groups split up and stay separated across scenes. If you have to write a scene with a bunch of characters, find ways for everyone to chime in and stay relevant in the conversation, instead of disappearing for pages of script only to pop up later and surprise the listener.

Dialogue is Important

Having good dialogue is central to having a good audio drama. You can get away with some amount of stilted conversation in a medium where that conversation isn't being said out loud (like a novel), but in audio drama we don't have that luxury.

Three things can make a conversation feel off. The first is what's being said (writing). The second is *how* it's being said (acting). The third is *when* it's being said (dialogue editing).

Let's take this exchange:

```
Robert: Hey dude, how's it going?

Sarah: Not so great, I slept through my alarm
again. Phone battery died overnight.

Robert: Are you gonna get a new phone?

Sarah: Think I have to, or else I'll be
writing apology letters to my profs all
semester.
```

Some of the writing isn't grammatically correct, but it reflects how people talk. When you read it, you probably imagined intonations for most of the lines, like "not so great" said unhappily or "I'll be writing apology letters to my profs all semester" said in a joking tone to lighten the mood.

But what if it was written like this?

Robert: Hello, how is it going?

Sarah: It is not going very well. I slept through my alarm again, because my phone battery died overnight.

Robert: Are you going to get a new phone?

Sarah: I think I have to, or else I will be writing apology letters to my professors all semester and they will be mad.

Or acted like this?

Robert: [quietly] Hey dude, how's it going?

Sarah: [loud and happily] No so great, I slept through my alarm again. Phone battery died overnight.

Robert: [angrily] Are you gonna get a new phone?

Sarah: [in tears] Think I have to, or else I'll be writing apology letters to my profs all semester.

Or edited in the dialogue cut like this?

Robert: Hey dude, how's it -

Sarah: Not so great, I slept through my alarm again. Phone battery died overnight.

[A long pause]

Robert: Are you gonna-

Sarah: Think I have to, or else I'll be writing apology letters to my profs all semester.

Robert: -get a new phone?

The answer is that all of these exchanges would feel off. I've taken each example to an extreme here; most scenarios where dialogue feels off would not be so exaggerated or obvious. But if your dialogue seems stilted, investigate these three likely contributors to it.

Ultimately, you want your dialogue to feel natural and not read off of a script. While part of this happens during recording and post-production, the bulk of it happens during the script writing phase.

You can always test the dialogue you've written by reading it out loud yourself, or asking some friends to join you. If it feels unnatural, go back to the drawing board. One of the easiest ways to improve in how you write dialogue is by listening to other conversations. How does this "real" dialogue flow? What grammatically incorrect phrases slip in? Where are the ums and uhs? It's eavesdropping with a purpose*.

***if you're caught eavesdropping, DO NOT tell them I sent you!**

Audio is Intimate

When you listen to a podcast, you feel like you're sitting next to the people talking. This intimacy holds for both fiction and nonfiction podcasts! In nonfiction chat-casts, a listener can feel like the hosts are their friends and that they're part of the conversation. In fiction, a listener can feel connected to the characters in a similar way. There's an element of being put directly into the scene that is different from the page, stage, or screen.

As a writer, you can take advantage of this fact. Small moments, like a sigh or under-breath whisper, can stand out. You can build moments of silence where you only hear a character breathe (this can be great for building tension in horror shows). Actors can play with a grounded and realistic acting style that would be overshadowed on the screen and stage. This isn't to say you have to work in low key moments into your script, but rather that you *can*.

But intimacy in audio goes beyond quiet moments having their time to shine. If you use a framing device, and have characters speak to whatever's recording, a listener will feel like the characters are speaking to them. If a character leaves a voicemail to someone, it's easy for a listener to put themselves in the place of the person getting a voicemail. Two characters having a discussion? Well now we've circled back to how it feels listening to nonfiction chat-casts. When you're not sitting back and watching people have a conversation, you feel like you're part of it instead.

Don't be afraid to build in quiet moments of monologues or dialogues into your script. These can be great opportunities to explore or develop characters and allow your audience to bond with them.

Don't Forget the Plot

This seems like obvious advice, but many first-time audio drama writers seem to get wrapped up in their characters and forget about the rest. Your scripts *can* be character-driven instead of plot-driven. In fact, audio drama is a medium where character-driven episodes thrive. You can get away with long scenes of characters talking to each other that would drag on screen. But balance is important; within your character-heavy scenes, you should have something happening.

Some character-driven audio dramas include:

- *Absolutely No Adventures*
- *Love & Luck*
- *Travelling Light*
- *The Bright Sessions*
- *Stories From Ylelmore*

Sidequesting is a heavily character-driven audio drama. In fact, the entire premise centers around avoiding the main plot. But as the name suggests, there's no shortage of side plots to be found in this audio drama. In each episode, the main character visits a new town and meets a new person who has a new problem. Their problems never have world-shattering implications. Maybe someone's basket of apples went missing, or a witch and her neighbor are in an argument, or a gnome needs help finding his way home. The audience knows that the basket of apples will be found, the witch's argument will be resolved, and the gnome will make it home. But they're invested in seeing how these problems will be solved, and they enjoy getting to know the new character along the way.

This is what I mean when I say you need a balance between character and plot in your audio drama. No matter the type of story, you need stakes to drive the narrative forward. It can be low stakes, but it cannot be *no* stakes. In order for your audience to be invested in what happens to your characters, there needs to be an opportunity for something to happen.

You Don't Need a Framing Device

A framing device provides an in-universe reason for the audio to exist. Examples of framing devices include phone calls, audio diaries, found footage, security tapes, radio transmissions, and more. A framing device can be useful to explain away bad audio quality, but it also restricts what the story can include.

For example, *What Will Be Here* could only have a few scenes where the in-universe recorder was accidentally turned on, because the more times it happened, the more difficult it was to justify. The likelihood of a recorder in a backpack turning on and catching an interesting and plot relevant conversation is low, so doing this in the podcast required the audience to suspend their disbelief at these odds. I've found most audiences are willing to do some level of suspension of disbelief, but leaning on that suspension of disbelief too often is weak writing. Eventually, all you've got is plot holes.

If you find yourself having to jump through hoops to justify why or how something was recorded, you're allowed to ditch the framing device entirely. Try to remove the framing device in the drafting process if it's possible, as audiences can feel cheated if the rules of the universe change for no discernable in-plot reason. Alternatively, create that in-plot reason for the change! A new season can also stand as an acceptable excuse to change formats.

I recommend having a reason to use a framing device in your story instead of jumping to it as an easy way to utilize an audio format. "Weird town radio host" is a trope because so many creators listened to *Welcome to Night Vale* and wanted to do it too, without any reason beyond that. "Archivist makes supernatural recordings" is a trope because so many creators listened to *The Magnus Archives* and wanted to do that. Your choice of a framing device should go beyond "well, it seemed to work for this podcast I liked."

For example, I chose a framing device for *What Will Be Here* to emulate the Voyager golden record. The audio drama itself centers around the making of this recording and the building of the rocket to launch it into space. At the very end of the show, the audience hears the rocket launch. I wanted to give the audience the experience of listening to a recording from another time. In essence, the listener is who the characters are speaking to. Without the framing device, there would be no "you" for the characters to talk to. With the framing device, the intimacy of characters talking directly to the listener was possible.

Joy to the World follows the radio transmissions of an astronaut alone on the International Space Station on

Christmas Eve. We hear a few solo transmissions from Joy, but the bulk of the show is people on earth talking back to her via radio. Because the show is about making connections with strangers, having the audio consist entirely of those transmissions made sense for the story.

Your reason for using a framing device can be simpler than these examples. Maybe you just want to record on a bad mic or write a story that's entirely voicemails. That's okay! But you don't have to force a framing device, and in many cases, it can be easier to do without.

Some audio dramas *without* a framing device:

- *Absolutely No Adventures*
- *VALENCE*
- *Tales of the Echowood*
- *Inn Between*
- *Re: Carmilla*
- *Sidequesting*

Ultimately, framing devices in audio drama work the same as in any other medium. When used with purpose, a framing device can have a great effect. When used willy-nilly, it can fall flat. Consider exploring how framing devices are used in other mediums if you're considering one for your show.

Movies with a framing device:

- *The Blair Witch Project*

- *V/H/S*
- *Lake Mungo*
- *Host*

TV shows with a framing device:

- *The Office*
- *What We Do In The Shadows*
- *24*
- *Parks and Rec*

Timing Matters

Your script(s) should be finished before you cast actors. It's usually considered rude to cast voice actors and leave them hanging while you finish writing. It's best practice to write in batches, one season at a time. This way you can complete writing, then editing, then recording (and so on), instead of trying to write one episode while you record another and sound design a third. This also allows you to get to know your actors over the season and then write *for* them in the next season. Writing seasons at a time prevents early episodes from being "locked in" down the road. It leaves you the option to modify the beginning of your show after you write the end, sneak in foreshadowing, and remove plot threads that didn't go anywhere. In short, your show will be better if you write it before you start recording.

Content Warnings

Something to consider near the end of the script-writing process is compiling a list of content warnings for each episode of your show. Content warnings, also called trigger warnings or content notes, give a heads-up to potentially upsetting content that an episode covers. Sometimes they are read at the top of an episode as part of the introduction, and other times they are placed in the show notes.

Content warnings enable audience safeguarding by giving both a warning of the distressing content and the time for a listener to disengage before hearing it. It puts the choice of interacting with the content into the hands of the individual and empowers them to take care of themself, if needed.

It's impossible to give a warning for every single thing that could potentially be upsetting to any single person — and no one expects this. What *is* expected is to provide warnings for basic sensitive content.

If you're not sure what "basic sensitive content" includes, I recommend referencing the television content rating system. Generally, a good rule of thumb is "if you're asking yourself if you should include a content warning for something, you should include a content warning for that thing."

Here are some examples of often overlooked content warnings for audio:

- Audible gore
- Gunshots

- Sirens
- Honking
- Sounds of a car crash

These are things that don't stand out on their own in a written format, but can be distressing for a listener, especially while driving.

Audible gore (think the tearing of limbs, slicing of flesh, or the sounds of gruesome body horror) is often covered in warnings about violence, but especially for shows with a narrator, it can be helpful for a queasy listener to know there will be sounds to go along with it.

Gunshots are another sound covered by the term "violence" (often specified to "gun violence") but knowing that there will be the sound of gunshots helps a listener prepare for them. It also helps a listener know that the gunshots they hear are not happening in real life. For people that have experienced gun violence, hearing a gunshot can be triggering in a way that a narrator saying "then she aimed and took a shot" is not. Gunshots can also be very startling!

Sirens, honking, and the sounds of a car crash are included in this list because many people listen to podcasts while driving, and knowing that these sounds are not happening outside their car is important. These types of warnings are also helpful for people listening while they walk outside. These types of content warnings are less about distressing content, and more about knowing what is (and isn't) actually happening.

By including content warnings, you build trust with your audience. It's almost a form of checking in with your listener and going, "you good to hear this?" — they'll know you're looking out for their wellbeing and appreciate the gesture.

If you're worried about spoilers, you don't need to read the content warnings at the beginning of the episode or put them at the top of the show notes. You can read "content warnings are in the show notes" at the beginning of the episode and/or put the content warnings at the bottom of the show notes. What matters, ultimately, is making the content warnings accessible to those who need them. Because some people absolutely will.

Script Formatting

Script formatting in audio drama is flexible. Some folks utilize formal screenwriting formatting, and others wing it on Google Docs (I am the latter). Regardless of how you choose to format your script, you should keep things consistent.

There are lots of options for script writing programs, both free and paid. Many first-time creators use Google Docs for the simplicity and ease of sharing. Others are drawn to screenwriting programs like Celtx, Scriviner, Writer Duet, or Final Draft. Some use Word or Pages because it came free with their computer. If you're writing alone, there's not a correct answer here, and I recommend poking around until you find a program you're comfortable with. Especially if you're just starting out, you don't need fancy tools. When it comes to sharing a final script with your production crew, sending it out as a view-only Google doc link or PDF is standard for audio drama. If you're co-writing a script, use software your partner can also access.

You should write which character is speaking before the dialogue lines. The common ways of doing this are:

CHARACTER: I am saying something!

Or:

<u>CHARACTER</u>
I am saying something!

Do not under any circumstances format your audio drama script like a novel or short story. C*haracter says, "I am saying something!"* is not a script. Your voice actors may quit, and they would be fully in the right to do so.

Sound effects should be separated out from actor dialogue. My preference is to format them like:

[SFX: a loud crash]

Brackets are used to distinguish it from dialogue, and "SFX:" allows for a sound designer to use ctrl-f to jump to all sound effects. It's not out of line to use "ENV:" or "AMB:" instead of "SFX:" to notate environment ambiance sounds. Other ways of noting sound effects include:

(a loud crash)

a loud crash

EXT: these are the outside sounds

INT: these are the inside sounds

These would be separate from dialogue with a paragraph break and distinguished with parenthesis or italics. A sound designer would have to comb through the script to make sure no sounds are skipped, instead of using a ctrl-f.

The goal with script formatting is to make it clear what is dialogue and what is not, allowing actors to record their lines easily and sound designers to sound design easily. This should be possible without extra highlighting or fancy fonts.

Sound effects that the actor is providing, such as a laugh or cough, should be placed within the actor dialogue. Actors are more likely to miss notes like "SFX: Character shouts in alarm" because they're focused on dialogue instead. Here are some examples.

Artemis: [with a laugh] Yeah, that really happened!

Dorian: [whispering] Be careful, they're gonna hear us...

Nox: [small coughing fit] I swear I'm not contagious.

Gregor: [shouts in alarm]

For projects where recording will be asynchronous (meaning actors record on their own time without a director present), bracketed notes can be used as directorial notes. Notations like these can be used to make sure actors approach scenes with the desired energy, and reduce the need for retakes.

Artemis: [teasing] I can't believe you!

Dorian: [timidly] Is that the best option we've got?

Nox: [angry] You told me you'd be home three hours ago!

Gregor: [has something to hide] I have nothing to hide.

It's up to you as a writer to decide when notes like this are needed. Avoid putting them on every line, or when the context makes characters' emotions clear. If you're planning on recording live with your actors, and especially if someone else will be directing your script, notes like these aren't usually necessary. We'll touch on this more in the chapter on recording.

Here are some script snippets from my own productions:

Rory: [only a little awkwardly] Greetings!

Gate Guard: State your name and purpose for entering.

Rory: I am . . . uhhh . . . Jimothy, here to sell my wares at your market. These are my traveling companions and fellow merchants.

Gate Guard: Thank you. You four may enter.

[SFX: Gate opens, footsteps as they walk through it]

Fig: [quietly, somewhat relieved] That was easy. [pause] This way.

[SFX: Footsteps. 4 pairs.]

Fig: [quietly] annnd here we are

[SFX: Closet door opens]

Astrid: [quietly] You ready, Rory?

Rory: [Mostly quietly, but containing excitement] Oh yeah.

[SFX: Footsteps as three people go into the closet, then the closet door closes.]

<u>JULES</u>

Hello. Hello. Hi. Hi! Jules here! I'm working on a little time capsule project to send a message to the future, and these recordings are part of it! This recorder? Our payload. And there's a whole group of us working on it!

SFX: Footsteps under as JULES moves around the space.

<u>JULES</u>

We have a team of 5, including myself. Everyone has a different specialty! I love seeing what they do. Being a part of this project is so exciting.

SFX: JULES'S voice begins to echo as she enters a new space.

<u>JULES</u>
Oh hey, there's one of them right now. Armani! Armani come here!

SFX: Footsteps as JULES approaches ARMANI.

<u>ARMANI</u>
Jules! That is not how you hold a mic! There is a handle, hold it by the handle!

<u>JULES</u>
I am! This is the handle!

<u>ARMANI</u>
No! That is NOT it. Give it here!

<u>JULES</u>
I got it-

SFX: Muffled shuffling noises as ARMANI takes the mic from JULES and shows them how to handle it properly.

<u>ARMANI</u>
There. That's better.

Sounds of an approaching skirmish, heard through closed elevator doors. Two humans, six zombies. The humans are running, getting closer to the elevator door. The zombies follow, groaning and trying to get to the humans. CAMERON stalls in their approach, hitting a zombie with a baseball bat.

1 CAMERON
Ah! Ugh! Oof!

Meanwhile, DAKOTA rushes towards the elevator.

2 CAMERON (CONT'D)
Dakota, there's no way that elevator works!

3 DAKOTA
This building has power! It might! We're out of options here, Cameron, unless you think you can clear the stairs.

4 CAMERON
Yeah, that's not happening. AUGH! Get off!

Cameron has a particularly rough scuffle with a zombie, hitting it with the bat. Dakota presses the elevator button furiously.

5 DAKOTA

(muttering to self)

Come on, come on, come on, just give me this.

There is a ding and the door opens. Everything now comes through clearly.

6 DAKOTA (CONT'D)

IT'S OPEN!

7 CAMERON

ONE SECOND!

8 DAKOTA

This is our only exit!

9 CAMERON

They're all on my tail here!

10 DAKOTA

So HURRY!

11 CAMERON

I am!

```
DAKOTA and CAMERON enter the elevator with
extraordinary effort, pushing and hitting
the zombies back as the door closes.
```

You'll notice that the formatting is slightly different for all of these. But despite their differences, each script is clear and understandable. That's what matters!

More examples of scripts can be found in the appendix, if you'd like to compare writing styles and formatting.

Script Editing

Basically, all editing advice ever also applies here. It can be supremely helpful to have someone else look over your script, especially if that person is familiar with audio drama. Finding a writing (or creator) community can also help you develop your scripts. You can organize swaps where each person provides feedback on the other's work.

Hearing your words read out loud will likely reveal stilted dialogue you want to change. Some writers do table reads with their friends before casting and producing their script. When doing table reads or recording sessions with your actors, it's generally permissible to change a word or two, but you should consider your script more or less set in stone when sending it to actors. It's frowned upon to do major script changes after recording, especially when you're not paying actors per hour.

It's important to not only edit each episode on their own, but the show as a whole. Like with any serialized media, you're managing two arcs at once: an arc for each episode and an arc for each season. Maybe you're also managing an additional arc for the show as a whole, spanning past a single season. Keep these overall arcs in mind when you edit.

Chapter 5

Beginning Production

You've got your idea, and you know what you want to get out of it. You have a sense of how that idea might need to change based on the constraints of the medium, your abilities, or your budget. You also have a rough understanding of the different roles you may need to fill and how to best present yourself. It's time to dive into the details of production.

Finding Community

If you're new to audio drama, it can be hard to know where to look for collaborators. Who can you reach out to for advice? Where are the creator communities located? What are the social expectations defining interaction? This is a difficult thing to write about because the space is constantly changing. I can tell you that in 2026, there are a few great Discord servers to join and a budding group of creators interacting on the "audio drama" tag on Tumblr, but who knows how long any of that will last. My advice for this section will be somewhat generalized in an attempt to prevent it from becoming dated.

The first thing you must do is listen to other indie audio dramas. You can start by searching podcast apps or search engines, but the best way to find new audio dramas is seeing what other shows are recommending. Many productions put trailers for other shows at the end of their episodes or share them directly on their feed.

The next thing you can do is follow your favorite productions on social media. You'll have to search around on whatever site you use (not all shows will have accounts on all sites), but once you've found a few, you can see who those shows are interacting with and increase your follow list. Branch out to following the creators themselves and whoever those people are interacting with. See what they're talking about. Engage. Learn. If you like something that an audio drama is doing, share it! Every creator loves hearing good things about their work.

Finding community also means finding resources. There's a near-endless stream of "How To" articles, free assets, and general advice available online. It can be hard to separate the good from the useless, but seeing what resources creators share and recommend is supremely helpful. Don't feel like you have to wait to be personally recommended a resource to use it, though. Searching them out on your own can yield gems you'll be able to share.

The more you interact with your fellow creators in public spaces, the more likely it is you'll find yourself in semi-public spaces akin to Discord servers or Facebook groups. These form as a way for creators to interact in places shielded from the bulk of their audience; not strictly private, but not anywhere a normal listener will stumble across. In these spaces, techniques and processes are talked about more openly. Plans for future episodes may be shared, or questions that reveal those plans may be asked. Cross promos might be traded, and the industry as a whole may be speculated about.

When reaching out to other creators to network, a great place to start is by showing them you've listened to their show. This can be as simple as posting about it on social media, or starting an email or DM with a few compliments. Especially if you're asking for advice or a favor, showing that you've done your research will go far. However, it's important to remember that you shouldn't feel entitled to someone's time just because you've listened to or like their show. Even if you've done your research, a creator isn't under any obligation to reply to you.

If you're asking others for advice, keep it simple and quick, or pay them for a consultation. In general, you should give more than you get, respect boundaries, and avoid gossip. If you want to hop on a call with someone to "pick their brain" (or something that will only benefit you, and not them), pay them for their time.

If cold emailing other creators is intimidating, I recommend being active in creator groups instead. You'll be able to get to know other creators, and potentially form genuine friendships with them. Regardless, once you've brushed shoulders with someone for a while in a group, it should be less intimidating to reach out privately, because you both know each other.

There will likely be multiple semi-public spaces with different subsets of creators. Even on fully public social media, you'll find (less defined) groups interacting with each other. The audio drama community is large enough that it's never going to be one single community. It tends to be a bunch of smaller spheres overlapping in different places. Two people can be part of "the audio drama community" and never know about each other, let alone interact.

These parallel communities are an asset. For example, if you end up in a space with someone you don't like, it's easy to find another space to inhabit. You can also hang out in multiple spaces and get different advice from different types of people. But as a result of these parallel communities, it's difficult to make sweeping statements about "the audio drama community." I bet you'll find *an* audio drama community once you start looking, but don't think it's the only one. When I refer to "the audio drama community," I'm mostly talking about a collective of audio drama creators, wherever they may be.

Like any other community, drama will occasionally erupt and spread around. Sometimes this drama will be stupid. Other times it will be rooted in important criticisms of shows or creators, such as "this person plagiarized my work" or "this person physically threatened me." It's important that you don't immediately brush off call-outs (or call-ins) from creators (and especially marginalized creators) as drama. Disagreements and friction are occasionally required to improve the industry.

But sometimes it really is just drama, and my recommendation for that is to not engage.

Setting Rates

Money is always a contentious topic, and it's no different in the audio drama sphere. The fact that volunteer shows share their work in the same space as industry-backed productions makes this all the more complicated. Imagine if community theater troupes were performing alongside high-budget Broadway shows for the same audience! Some choice words might be exchanged backstage.

There isn't an easy line dividing "hobby" from "professional." What makes a show "indie" is a constant point of debate. Here's what different levels might look like and how easily a show's status can change:

- A group of students or online friends make a podcast together. No one is paid and no income is expected.
- A showrunner is doing their own writing and production, but working with volunteer actors. No one is paid and no income is expected. Hobby . . . for now. They might grow their show enough to get ad revenue, and start paying their voice actors.
- A producer duo pays freelance cast and crew small stipends out of their own pocket. In this scenario, usually little to no income is expected. There might be a Patreon, but money made always goes into the show. Maybe their Patreon takes off, and they can increase the stipends paid to freelancers. They might decide to use additional funds to grow the show, or pocket it to pay bills.
- A showrunner is doing a small crowdfunding campaign: freelancers are paid small stipends from the fundraiser instead of from the showrunner. The showrunner isn't paid. All money made goes into the show. For season two, they might do a bigger crowdfunding campaign.
- A showrunner does a larger crowdfunding campaign. Rates are better but not high, and the showrunner makes a little income (or invests those funds into other parts of the show, for example

having a bigger marketing budget). As the show makes more money, rates paid to cast and crew increase proportionally.

- A production team does a large crowdfunding campaign. They pay industry rates to their cast and crew but make little money themselves. As the show makes more money, the producers begin to pay themselves more, but they sink too much time into production for it to technically be a fair rate.
- A showrunner is making enough money from their well established show to quit their day job and do it full time, though their pay isn't quite industry standard. They only hire voice actors and manage production themself.
- A production team establishes a company to produce audio dramas. They hire former freelancers full time, but pay rates well below industry standard.
- A production team establishes a company to produce audio dramas, and with the help of investors is able to pay industry rates to their team.
- A showrunner pitches a concept to a production house and receives funding. Everyone, including the showrunner, is paid industry rates.

Where do you draw the line separating "hobby" from "professional"? Is it when any income is made at all? Is it when industry rates are met? Somewhere in between? Let's angrily debate about it online!

Or . . . we can accept that such a distinction is meaningless — and furthermore, that it can be hard to tell a creator's situation from the outside.

Audio dramas can be made with a lot of funding or on a shoestring budget, which means that rates for audio drama production can be high, low, or nothing at all. A lot of bickering can occur when creators paying different rates look over their shoulders and see the other person doing something different. Producers running volunteer hobby projects see cries for higher pay as attacks, even when those cries for higher pay are directed at people paying voice actors five times more than their sound designers. Producers paying reasonable stipends might scoff at volunteer casting calls or judge low crew rates, when they should understand that hobby projects aren't a threat to their productions or income.

When the rates vary so much, how do you set your own? How do you know what's fair? Here are some things to keep in mind:

If you are getting revenue for your show, you should be paying the people involved.

There can be exceptions! A volunteer show might donate their ad revenue to charity, or a group of friends might decide to use merch income to commission character art. However, everyone involved in the production should be on board for these situations.

Have an idea of how much time each role takes, and divide stipends accordingly.

Sound designing an episode takes much, much longer than recording it, and a lead actor is probably recording longer than a minor actor. If you have multiple people doing the same role (such as two sound designers), you should be paying them the same rate for the same work. If you have people in the same role but doing different amounts of work (such as a lead sound designer and a supporting sound designer), the person doing more work should get more pay.

As your show income increases, pay should increase as well.

There's no easy answer to *how* pay should increase. It's a balance between investing in the show with marketing or more ambitious production, and paying your team more per hour. Back pay is rarely, if ever, expected. The best thing to do is communicate with your team about show income increases and make sure they're on board. This can be as simple as, "we're making $200 more a month on ads, so I can pay everyone $10 more per episode." As showrunner, you can decide what to do, but I recommend checking with your team to ensure it is fair.

Being transparent with your cast and crew about your budget will minimize issues.

In general, communicating with your team is the right call. You're allowed to ask, "Is this fair?" as long as you can accept no for an answer. Share your budget, check in with your cast and crew, and reevaluate if needed.

There's no simple answer here. Approach pay rates with honesty and integrity, ask other creators what they're able to pay, compare your rates to the local cost of living, and see if there are indie rate guides online applicable to your situation. As your audio drama gets more revenue, you should strive to meet industry rates for your team and pay everyone a livable wage — yourself included!

Volunteer Productions

If you're doing a volunteer show, chances are some cast and crew members may "level up" and switch to only paid work. The longer your audio drama runs, the more likely this is to happen. Asking for volunteer work also decreases the pool of creatives interested in participating (for example, you'll have fewer auditions for an unpaid role than for a paid role). Some people can't afford to work for free, and others don't have the time to volunteer. But many people do both!

When it comes to crew roles in an all-volunteer audio drama, you're likely to be working with less experienced creatives looking to build their resume. I've noticed it's usually easy to find volunteer voice actors and writers, but finding audio editors willing to work for free is much more difficult. If you're a producer running a volunteer show and not planning on dialogue editing or sound designing, you will likely have to pay someone to fill those roles.

The Pros of a Volunteer Production:

- You don't have to deal with money, which means no fundraising, taxes, or payment processor fees.
- The team working on the show is doing it because they're passionate about it.

- It's easy to keep the project as a fun hobby, which decreases the chances of burnout.

The Cons of a Volunteer Production:

- You can't make the same time demands of a volunteer crew as one that you pay.
- Difficulty in filling roles like Dialogue Editor or Sound Designer.
- Usually means working with less experienced cast and crew.
- Often requires a longer production schedule.
- Cast and crew members are more likely to drop out of the project.

Budgeting and Payroll

We've already covered how much rates can vary in indie audio drama, so this section won't cover the numbers side of a budget, but rather what costs to expect and some tools for tracking them.

Here's a list of potential costs for audio drama production:

- website hosting and domain fees
- RSS feed hosting
- microphone and audio equipment
- audio editing software

- sound effect packs
- cover art commission
- theme music commission
- stickers and business cards
- crowdfunding fees
- cast and crew payments
- transcription costs

These are all *potential* costs because many can be done without or found for free. It's possible to host a website for free, though you will have to pay for a custom domain if you want one. Some RSS feed hosts are free, others are inexpensive, and yet others (with fancy bells and whistles) will be more costly. You can get away with your phone's mic or a cheap external mic, though I don't recommend it; investing in a good microphone is one of the better ways to spend your money.

Recording or editing can be done in a free program like Audacity, a less expensive program like Reaper, or a more expensive program like ProTools. Sound effects can be bought, or found for free on Freesound, or made yourself. You could create your own cover art using free stock images or Canva assets instead of commissioning one. Likewise, for theme music, you can utilize public domain music or create your own. Physical goods will always cost money, but are not necessary to create an audio drama. A volunteer show will not have crowdfunding fees or cast and crew payments. You can make your own transcript instead of paying someone to do it.

This is all to say, you get to decide how expensive your audio drama is going to be. There's no correct answer.

I recommend that all showrunners track both income and expenses for their audio drama, even if they're small. You can learn a lot about what you're paying for production and evaluate if you're getting your money's worth. Additionally, if you're based in the US, having all your expenses and income laid out for the year in one place should make your life significantly easier when it comes to filing taxes, especially if your audio drama is a business.

I utilize a free budgeting template on Notion for my expenses. It allows me to tag each item (for example, "ad revenue", "voice actors", "award fees", etc.) and filter based on those tags. This allows me to know exactly how much money has been sent to the cast and crew, and how much I've spent on other goods for the show. Notion isn't the only budget tracking software; you can do it in an Excel spreadsheet if you want something simple, or any number of other websites if you want something more complicated.

I use a similar labeling system in my email inbox, tagging all receipts and payment confirmations so that if I need to go back and confirm something, it's easier to do so. Usually, I'm checking my Notion budget to see what I've paid, though.

In the US, productions commonly pay cast and crew with online money wiring or transfer services like PayPal. It doesn't matter which payment processor you use, as long as your cast and crew members are okay with it. If you can pay them in multiple ways, consider giving them the option for which to use. Everyone has their own preferences for what's best.

I recommend collecting your cast and crew's payment information near the start of production and keeping it in one place, such as a spreadsheet. If you're sending recurring payments (instead of a single lump sum), track each payment interval as well. Sometimes being a showrunner is just managing a bunch of Excel documents, and that's especially the case when it comes to budgeting.

Making a Schedule

Audio dramas vary in how long they take to make based on the show itself and who is producing it. When you make your own production schedule, you should account for how long it takes *your team specifically* to make an episode. If you're coming at this for the first time, my suggestion would be to produce the first episode and use that experience to build the schedule for the rest of the episodes.

Here's a ballpark estimate for how long certain steps might take:

Writing: You know better than me how fast you write. I usually give myself a month per episode, but I know writers who have made their whole show in a week. If you're not sure how long you need to write, see how long it takes to write the first episode of your show and use that as a benchmark. If you're able to write the entirety of your show before going into production, take advantage of this. If you run into writer's block, you won't have to stress about holding everything up. When working with a writer's room, get everyone's feedback on the schedule before implementing it.

Pre-Production Prep: After writing and before casting, I recommend penciling in at least a month to finalize everything else you need before heading into production. Use this time to do final edits, work out your title and cover art, build a website, claim social media handles, and plan the rest of your production schedule. Basically, get your ducks in a row before you involve more people in the project. If you're a busy person, give yourself at least two months so you're not rushed between audio drama and everything else you've got going on.

Casting: I recommend two weeks for creating the casting call, three weeks of having the call open, two weeks for listening to auditions, and one week for onboarding actors. You can use the time while the call is open to finish the last of your pre-production prep, or just take a little break. You'll probably need it!

Recording: I recommend giving yourself 2–3 weeks per episode if you're doing asynchronous recording, and 1–2 weeks per episode if you're doing spaced out live recording. Voice actors typically won't mind recording two episodes a month on their own, or meeting weekly or bi-weekly for regular sessions. If you're recording multiple episodes at once, I suggest allowing a minimum of 90 minutes to record a 30-minute episode.

Audio Editing: I recommend expecting your dialogue editor to take about 2–3 weeks to edit a 30-minute episode. Provide them more time if there are a lot of characters. Usually when an audio drama is recorded live, you can plan for less time in the dialogue edit as well.

Sound Design: I recommend giving your sound designer 2–4 weeks to sound design a 30-minute episode. Give them more time if it's a longer or more sonically complicated episode. You can get away with less time if the sound design is minimal or simple.

Final Touches: I recommend giving yourself at least two weeks between an episode's sound design completion and its release. Use this time to make the show notes and finish the transcript for the episode (more on both of these later). You can also use this time to prepare any social media posts about the episode in advance. If you're able to produce all the episodes in a season before you start releasing them, do it. In this scenario, give yourself a month to do these final tasks.

Crowdfunding: If you're planning to crowdfund, give yourself at least two months to prepare your crowdfund, run the campaign, and then fulfill rewards. Ideally, this isn't done in tandem with other production work. If it is, allocate buffer time in your schedule. Crowdfunding is a full-time job, and you will find yourself pulled away from production to manage the campaign.

Chapter 6

Casting

Once you've found your corner of the audio drama community, you should have an idea of where to post cast and crew calls (or at least an idea of who to ask). But what does such a call look like? Let's break it down, with casting calls first.

Casting Call Formatting

My favorite casting calls are written up in Google Docs. PDFs come as a close second, but these can be difficult for those who use screen readers. Screen readers are a technology that allows people who are blind or low-vision to use the computer. It reads what's present on a screen out loud. When your casting call isn't compatible with screen readers, it makes casting people with visual impairments, dyslexia, or anyone else utilizing this technology more difficult.

Please don't only post your casting call as a series of images. Not only are these impossible for screen readers to read, your text isn't copy/pasteable, and folks who need to change text size, color, or font to read it won't be able to. Images are great to post on social media and to catch people's attention, but consider including a link to a Google Doc (or the text on your website) as well. If you're using Google Docs, make sure the link you share is view-only, not restricted or editable. You can check the permissions in an incognito window before you share the link.

On the document itself, you don't need to get fancy with formatting. It's more important to have clear, legible text than special colors or fonts. I like to include show art at the top of the casting call, but this is just a personal preference and not truly necessary. I've never had character art to share, but if you do, that could be worth including as well.

Before you list characters or audition lines, you should put information about your show, who you're looking for, and how auditions should be submitted. Something I find very useful as a voice actor is a quick breakdown at the top of the document, with information such as:

Title:
Project Type:
Union/Non-Union:
Length:
Recording Period:
Recording Location:
Compensation:
Audition Deadline:

You don't have to format it like this, of course, but if you're putting your information in a paragraph format, I recommend bolding the most important lines (such as deadline and payment). Keep your show information concise and to the point. Voice actors are reading lots of casting calls, often several ones after another. Make it easy for them.

Audition Instructions

After putting information about your show, follow up with the information voice actors should know for their audition.

These are some questions you should consider answering in your general information section:

- Do voice actors need to be in a specific location, or are you doing remote recording?
- How important is mic quality?
- Should voice actors say their name at the top of the audition?
- How many takes of each line should they record?
- How many characters can they audition for?
- Is improvisation welcome?
- What should they name the file?
- How should they submit their audition?
- What additional information should they send with their audition files?
- Are there any characters restricted to voice actors from certain demographics?
- Are there any content warnings for your show?

I want to briefly expand on that last question before moving on. If your show has dark or distressing themes, be up front about it in your casting call. Voice actors will want to know if they'll need to portray scenes of a violent or sexual natural. There are other themes, like death and grief, medical malpractice, or emotional abuse, that a voice actor may not want to be a part of. Listing content warnings on your casting call will give actors the choice to not engage with that content. If you don't include content warnings, you may have to recast an actor after they see the script.

You shouldn't ask actors (or anyone, for that matter!) why specific content is triggering for them, or why they need to not engage with it. This holds true beyond the casting process, for every aspect of production. Something like this is more likely to occur if you're making a horror audio drama, but it's not limited to that genre.

And generally, you don't need to worry about spoilers when you write content warnings in your casting call, because the majority of your audience won't be seeing it. If you're worried, you can say up front in the casting call that it contains spoilers for the show.

A note on voice pitch:

It is incredibly helpful for transgender, non-binary, and gender-nonconforming voice actors if you include a note indicating who they should audition for. This can be as simple or as complicated as you want to make it.

I'm not going to go too deep into this, but I'll use myself as an example. I am an AFAB (assigned Female at birth) non-binary voice actor who isn't on testosterone, which means most people think I sound like a girl, and most audio dramas cast me in female roles. However, I'm also comfortable voicing male and nonbinary characters, not just women. If you include a note saying you welcome voice actors to audition for any character they feel comfortable playing, I know that it won't be a waste of my time to audition for a male character. If you don't say that, I'll probably just audition for the female/non-binary characters because those roles are what I tend to land.

In short, voices don't have a gender. There are men with high voices, women with low voices, and people who sit outside the gender binary with all different pitches. If you want characters to have a specific voice pitch, then say so. Don't just put "this character is male" and then reject all auditions from trans men with high voices. Make your expectations clear.

I'd also invite you to think about your expectations and assumptions. If you want men with low voices for a character, ask yourself why. Look at why you wrote certain characters with certain genders, and evaluate how flexible their voice and pronouns might be.

Here's what I wrote for *Someone Dies In This Elevator*. This casting call had 25 roles, some with specific pronouns and some without. We ended up with a cast that was nearly 50% trans/non-binary.

"Some characters are written without a specific gender, while others have set pronouns. We invite transgender, nonbinary, and gender nonconforming individuals to audition for any character they would feel comfortable playing."

The *Sidequesting* casting call did not include specific characters, so I just included a note at the top that read *"People of color, trans people, queer people, and those from other marginalized groups are especially encouraged to audition."*

This is important to say because it's never "obvious" that you won't discriminate. Some marginalized people will have been turned away so much from auditions that they assume they can only audition for roles specific to their demographic. A note like this makes it clearer that your production is inclusive and values diversity.

But if you're not going to cast like this, don't say you are. For example: don't write "We invite transgender, non-binary, and gender nonconforming individuals to audition for any character they would feel comfortable playing" if you're not willing to cast these folks in the roles they feel comfortable playing.

Character Info

For this part of the call, you should consider listing character names, character pronouns, who the call is open for, a short description of the character, and number of lines that the character has.

Examples of the formatting I used for *Someone Dies In This Elevator* were:

Mary — This character uses she/her pronouns. Open casting. An artificial intelligence designed to calm and encourage Ezekiel through his various dates. 51 lines.

Wilson — Open casting, preference given to an older VA. A somewhat too relaxed member of an Architecture Firm Board. A very empathic and upbeat individual. 50 lines.

Tim — This character uses he/him pronouns. The role is only open to transmasculine voice actors. A younger man, the desk clerk. 28 lines.

Holly — Open casting. An experienced lawyer, prone to thinking about language to remain calm under pressure. 54 lines.

If you're looking for a certain type of voice, like for an older character, say so in the character description. Include whatever character information you think is important for voice actors to know. Don't feel like you have to fit the description into a single sentence or two, but keep it concise. If it isn't feasible to include the number of lines for each character, consider simply stating if they're leading, supporting, or an extra; possibly include episode count as well.

When picking audition lines, I look for a variety of emotions so that I can see an actor's range. I like having some lines where how the line is said is written out (ex: "kindly" or "crying") and some lines left open-ended for voice actor interpretation. I want to see how an actor takes instruction and what approaches they take without it. If I felt that context was necessary, I included that (ex: *Answering "Will it hurt?"*). Overall, I'm interested in how an actor sounds and how well they can portray the character.

If you have characters that engage in lots of back-and-forth banter, I'd recommend pulling a snippet of an exchange and including it in the audition. When you have audition audio, you can edit the exchange together and hear how your prospective actors sound together.

Here's an example of an exchange as an audition line. We had those who auditioned for Oak read only Oak's parts, and those auditioning for Holly read only Holly's part, but we provided the whole exchange under both characters for context.

```
HOLLY: (Grunts) The, uh, clasp comes undone
if I flex too much.
OAK: Allow me . . . oh dear. This is a fake
HOLLY: Fake? I shouldn't be surprised, yet…
OAK: The logo on the clock faces to the
left. Similar materials . . . guessing the
factory sold their defective units at a
discount.
```

For *Sidequesting*, I wasn't casting for specific characters, but rather collecting a pool of voice actors to cast from as I wrote. So for this show, I focused on providing lines that gave a range of emotions. I didn't plan on doing table reads for *Sidequesting*, so I was especially interested in how actors took scripted instruction (this is why all four lines have some sort of guidance).

This is what that call looked like:

Please give me your best read of these lines. Improvisation is welcome, but not required. You may send up to three different takes of each line. No specific accent is necessary, and I'd prefer you to use your natural voice.

1. [excitedly sharing information] It all comes from something. It all goes somewhere. Maybe that somewhere is another plane, but still . . .

somewhere. People say magic just happens, but nothing *just happens*. Everything has a cause.

2. [calm, reassuring] Deep breath. It's okay. Just think of blowing a candle out. [pause] There you go. That wasn't too bad, was it?

3. [grumpy, complaining to a friend] I wish someone would succeed in getting that darn sword, or that everyone would just give up and go home. I tell you, if another person brings their pet ogre into town, I'm going to lose it. I can't take this chaos much longer.

4. [accusatory] You're lying . . . I know it was you! The stolen wares were transported in a carriage with your seal on it. This very carriage, in fact! What do you have to say for yourself now?

A note on casting marginalized groups:

Please don't cast white actors as characters of color, and please don't cast cisgender actors in transgender roles.

If someone from a marginalized group comes to you with an issue about your casting call, please listen to them! I know that a wave of defensiveness may come over you if/when issues are brought up, but keep in mind that this person is doing you a favor by letting you know. Try to understand

their perspective. I promise it's not the end of the world (or your audio drama) if there's something untoward in your casting call. Just listen, fix it, apologize, and move on.

Casting with Intention

Something to keep in mind when creating the characters of your show and casting them is to do so with intention. Question your expectations and assumptions, and look critically at what sort of voices you want for each character. There is no singular right way to do this, so I'm going to use an example to discuss different ways to cast with intention.

Let's say you have an audio drama with some male characters, some female characters, and a robot that has a human voice but is not human (the robot uses it/its pronouns because it is an object). You split up the roles in your casting call to "male roles" and "female roles" and then . . . where does this robot go? Maybe you think to yourself, *I've always pictured this robot with a male voice. Let's put it in the male roles section and be done.*

First of all, something is apparent: there are no trans or nonbinary roles. In this situation, it would be important to say if you welcome trans people to audition. Would you be cool with a trans woman auditioning to play a cis woman? Without saying so up front, most people would guess not. You might miss out on auditions from this demographic (which, from experience, I know contains many talented voice actors).

But back to the example. Every role here is either a cis man or a cis woman — not necessarily bad, but in this situation, the robot has even been assigned to the "male" category. Why is that, I ask? So you might think, *yeah, I'm not actually attached to this robot having a male voice. Let's make this a nonbinary role.*

And now you've accidentally stumbled into a trope! Lots of creators have made non-human characters (like aliens, robots, or monsters) and decided that the gender binary need not apply only to these characters. Nonbinary people are tired of the implications that you can't be human and nonbinary, so that's not a great thing to do. If you're going to create a "Nonbinary Roles" section for this robot, it would be a good thing to have some nonbinary humans there as well.

But if this robot could have any voice, why not make it an open role? And while you're at it, why not look at the other human characters and see if any of them could be open roles too? There are a lot of scenarios where you want a character to have a specific gender. It's not a bad thing! What casting with intention means is you look at the gender you have for each character, and think about why you decided that gender for the character.

Is someone female because you wanted to show a woman in tech being an awesome scientist? Cool! Is someone male because they're the CEO and you just thought the CEO should be male? Less cool! That CEO could probably be a role with open casting. Or maybe, you thought of an interesting angle for the story if that CEO is nonbinary, or transmasc, or a cis woman — also great! Being intentional about your roles doesn't mean making them all open casting; it means having a reason why you're looking for a certain voice (or set of voices) or each one.

For our example above, what if this robot started the show as genderless and inhuman, but grew over time to connect more with humanity? What people start using he/him for this robot instead of it/its as they get to know it better and start to think of him as a friend? I think that would be compelling. That might be a good reason for the robot to be listed under "Male Roles" (though, of course, the question of "why not she/her pronouns?" is there still and should be something you can answer — maybe you want to be different from robots and AIs like Siri or Cortana, which are usually voiced by cis women.)

There is absolutely no one correct way to cast with intention; the whole idea is about the process, not the result. When you list a role in a casting call, take a moment to think about why you've written each piece of information you give about the character and the voice you want. You might find that you're limiting yourself from telling more interesting stories and casting more diverse actors.

Collecting Auditions

You've written your call, but how should people submit? To collect auditions, some shows ask voice actors to email them with their audition, often specifying a specific subject line to be used in the email. Others utilize a Google or Airtable form for submissions. Personally, I prefer the latter, but everyone's organization system is likely to be different, and you should follow whatever works for you.

I like Google/Airtable forms because you can specify exactly what information you want from actors, and the form will collect and organize all responses for you. Instead of combing through emails and downloading every audition, I had all responses automatically put in a spreadsheet and all audition files in a Google drive folder. It made sorting through the 500 auditions I got for one casting call far easier than it would've been otherwise.

You can also set up automatic email filters based on the subject line or content. I've never done this, but at minimum you could have all audition emails go to an "audition" folder, potentially different ones for each character. It will depend on the email program you use and how specific the filters can get. But if this sounds overwhelming to you, there's nothing wrong with manually sorting email auditions as you get them.

Forms I make usually ask for:

- Name
- Pronouns
- Email
- Which characters actors are auditioning for
- An upload of the audio files
- Confirmation that actors are not submitting an audition for a role restricted to a demographic they are not a part of

I'll also have optional questions for audio fiction experience, demo reel, any situations actors wouldn't feel comfortable acting in, and an open-ended catch-all question in case there's something else actors want to add.

Listening and Casting

Some people prefer to listen to auditions as they come in, and others prefer to wait until the call has closed to start listening. Either option is perfectly fine, but if you're listening to auditions as they're submitted, avoid early casting. Many voice actors build their audition schedule based on submission deadlines, and it's rude to abruptly close a call because it disrupts actors' planning. It also limits your acting pool: you might think you've found the perfect voice, but unless you wait until the end of your audition period, you'll never know if you could be missing an even more perfect voice. There's also a nonzero chance that someone could audition for a role you otherwise would have closed early, only to be the perfect fit for a *different* role you hadn't found the right fit for yet. If you're getting more auditions than you planned and fear you're going to be overwhelmed, give as much notice as possible before closing the casting call early. I recommend at least a week.

Casting calls are open for a wide range of time. I've seen last minute casting calls up for a day, and others up for a month or more. I've found that a few weeks are usually all that's required. There's a surge of auditions when a call opens, another surge when the call is about to close, and occasional spikes when the call is posted to various actor groups.

It's considered distasteful to put a role on a casting call and end up casting yourself in the role. This is because it's a waste of time for every actor who submitted for that role. In indie audio drama, showrunners and producers frequently lend their voices to the production, but they don't fill in for roles listed on their casting call. If an actor drops out of a role, I recommend hiring a different person who auditioned.

When going through auditions, many creators track the process with a spreadsheet. I'll put each role on its own sheet, each voice actor in a row, and leave comments on each audition as I listen. Once I've listened to all the auditions for a character, I'll create a shortlist, which is a subset of all the actors whose auditions I liked for a specific role.

I then re-listen to the shortlist auditions, add additional notes, and narrow it down. I like to create a shortlist for every role in the call before I begin any final decisions. Because voice actors may audition for multiple roles, I'll often end up in situations where the same voice actor is on multiple shortlists. Usually, I want to avoid casting one actor in two roles, and knowing the multiples as I narrow various lists down is quite helpful.

What should you listen for?

The first thing I do is listen for audio quality. I'm up front in my casting call that I expect a certain level of audio quality. I don't want background noise, clipping, echoes/reverb, or other distortion. People still submit with this anyway, which means my first pass of audition listening is weeding out all the actors whose mics and studios are not up to par. If you're collaborating with a sound designer on your audio drama, I recommend working with them to determine what is acceptable audio quality. Before you cast any voice actors, ensure the sound designer can work with their audio.

A quick aside: You may end up with a situation where your favorite actor for a role has less than stellar audio quality. It could be worth reaching out to the actor to see if they can improve their setup. Audio quality can only be improved so much in post, and you should avoid putting an unnecessary burden on your audio editor. Sometimes, you may have to pass on your first choice actor because of their audio quality. If this happens, it's okay to encourage them to audition for future projects.

No matter how you cast your audio drama, keep in mind that it's better to have all actors on a slightly subpar mic than most actors on a subpar mic and a few on a good one. The distinction of "suddenly, here's someone with excellent audio quality" will break immersion. An audio editor can only do so much to make audio recorded on different mics, in different rooms, sound like two people talking in the same place. We'll discuss this more in the section on recording practices.

Once I've done my pass for audio quality, I'm listening to see if the actor's voice matches the character. Sometimes I don't have an idea of what a character sounds like. Other times I'm looking for a specific vibe. Can I picture my character when I hear this voice? If not, they don't make it to the short list. This is the least technical pass of listening I do. There's no specific guidelines I follow — it's all based on feeling. If you follow the same steps as me, keep what I said about voice pitch in mind. Be aware of your expectations for what a character should sound like.

Next, I'll listen for acting skills. I'll have strategically included a tougher line in the audition, probably something emotional. I've also likely included something mundane. I've found that the emotional-mundane two line combo is a good litmus test for acting ability. New or untrained actors often struggle with one of the two. An emotional line might be over-acted, and a mundane line might come off stilted. It's not a perfect science, but I've found that it works well for me.

From these three passes, I'll end up with a shortlist of actors for each role. This list can be 2 to 10 people I think could be a good fit for the role. From there, I start looking at the cast as a whole. For example, I'll ensure that characters from the same location sound alike, especially if accents weren't specified in the call itself. I also want to make sure the voice for each character is distinct, and that they work together well.

If the voice actors for two different characters have similar voices, a listener will struggle telling those two characters apart. Have you ever watched a movie where two main characters looked a little too alike? It makes tracking the plot a lot more difficult because you can't tell who is doing what. It's important for the audience to know Character A from Character B. Even if two characters aren't in the same scene together, casting similar voices can lead listeners to question how the first character they met has ended up in this new location.

If your top audition for one character sounds too much like your top audition for another character, it's likely you'll have to cast your second choice for one of them. Sometimes you can't cast your favorite actor for a role, but rather someone else whose voice balances well within the show as a whole. Having variations in vocal pitch, tone, accent, inflection, and speed across the actors you cast will lead to a more vocally diverse production and help each character feel like a different person and sound distinct.

Some creators opt to run callbacks for the voice actors in their shortlist, especially when they want to test the chemistry of their potential leads. Callbacks aren't standard in audio drama, but they won't be unexpected for voice actors. Be upfront in your casting call document about the possibility and you won't run into issues. If emailing your whole shortlist at once for a callback, be sure to bcc the emails to keep their contact information private from the others on the email.

Casting is a lot of work, but I love it. You're building half the sound of your audio drama in that process (the other half will be coming from musicians and sound designers), and picking the people you'll be working closely with to bring your idea to life.

Rejection Emails

Once you know who you're casting, what do you do about the people you're not bringing aboard? Do you let them know? This is a hotly contested point in the voice acting sphere. Some people appreciate them. Others despise them. It is truly a no-win scenario.

The breakdown seems to occur between voice actors auditioning for a job and voice actors auditioning for fun. Professional or aspiring voice actors audition for many productions at a time, and don't want to deal with an influx of "no"; they only want to be contacted for a yes. Voice actors who do this for fun tend to audition for fewer productions, and would rather find out they haven't been cast from an email instead of seeing cast announcements on social media or coming across the show itself.

One way I have vanquished this no-win scenario is by asking everyone who submits an audition if they'd like to be notified if they are not cast. This was as simple as adding a question to my submission form and sorting my spreadsheet based on answers, collecting only the emails of those who wanted to be notified. If that sounds like too much work, I recommend simply stating in your casting call document if you plan on sending rejection emails or not, and letting actors decide for themselves if they want to audition.

If you are planning on sending rejection emails, you do not need to share the final cast in those emails. A simple "we went with someone else" will do. I've seen cast lists sent to all auditionees a few times, usually from creators with theater experience. This practice is frowned upon in the voice acting sphere. Let your rejected actors discover the final cast with the rest of your audience.

As with any bulk email, if you are batch-sending rejection emails, ensure you've bcc-ed the emails and not cc-ed the emails.

Closed Casting

You might not want to run a big casting call — many people don't. One option is to run a closed casting call, which involves creating an audition document but inviting specific people to apply instead of posting it to the general public. Actors typically don't mind cold emails with audition invitations. In fact, they're usually pretty happy about them. When sending cold emails, it can be helpful to let the actor know how you found them, especially if you got their contact info from someone else.

Another option is to simply inquire if an actor would be up for playing a role, no audition required. Actors also don't typically mind cold emails with role offers. Some may decline based on rate or schedule, but they likely won't be unhappy that you emailed. If you're running a small hobby project, there's no issue teaming up with a few friends to fill your cast. It can be a lot of fun! When casting directly, be sure to be upfront about your expectations, schedule, and time requirements. Do your best to avoid "scope creep," where you get a yes for one thing (say, 20 lines in an episode) and assume the person is in for more (say, a multi-episode appearance).

Bringing on Crew

When showrunners are looking for composers, sound designers, dialogue editors, etc., basically any role that is not "actor" or "showrunner," they might hold a crew call, or they'll query freelancers directly.

Crew calls differ from casting calls because there's no simple means of auditioning. Usually a crew call will ask for examples of previous work instead. A showrunner will then pick a few promising candidates and discuss further. Unlike with casting calls, it's more customary to send rejection emails to people who apply for crew calls (but certainly not required). My recommendation is that if you receive under a dozen applicants, let people know you're going with someone else.

Information in a crew call might look like:

Title:
Project Type:
Length:
Production Period:
Compensation:
Application Deadline:

Questions you should consider answering in your general information section include:

- What is the pay rate? (Is it per episode, per hour, a set stipend, or something else?)
- How should they apply?
- What additional information should they send with samples of their work?
- What will the production process look like?
- What will the production schedule be?
- Are there any content warnings for your show?

For Writers:

- Do you have an outline or show bible for them to use?
- What will script editing look like?
- What are the deadlines or timeline involved?

- How many rounds of script revision do you expect?
- Will writers oversee episodes, scenes, or dialogue for specific characters?
- Will writers be involved in making choices that affect the plot, including any additional seasons?
- Will writers be expected to edit any scripts?

For Audio Editors:

- Are you recording remotely? Is recording synchronous? *(More on these terms soon!)*
- Will you be picking takes, or will audio editors (or directors) be expected to do that?
- Are you looking for dialogue editors, sound designers, mixing and mastering, or a combo thereof?
- How many rounds of episode revision do you expect?

For Composers:

- Are you looking for intro/outro music, underscoring, transition music, or something else?
- What are examples of the type of music you're looking for?

For audio editors, if you plan to provide a sample for them to edit, please also provide a stipend for their time. Audio editing is much more time intensive than voice acting;

requesting a four line audition file is very different from requesting a two-minute edited audio file.

For writers, if you plan on asking them to write a sample episode (or portion thereof), please provide a stipend to them as well. This is for the same reason as before. If you're creating new work for potential crew members, you should compensate them for it.

Querying freelancers can be as simple as asking other creators who they're working with and if they know anyone open to work. Sometimes informal calls are posted in creator spaces: a simple "Hey, I'm looking for a sound designer, DM me if you're interested." Instead of being spelled out in the information section of a crew call, the above questions are answered in the course of a casual conversation. Most freelancers looking for work will have samples of their previous work at hand to share with you.

In general, it's best to state your budget and what you can pay instead of asking for rates. This is because budgets vary wildly within audio drama. Some productions pay less than $50 an episode, and others pay more than $50 per hour of work. Being up front with what rates you can work with will save both you and freelancers a lot of time. Don't take it personally if a freelancer turns down working with you because of the rate. Generally, more experienced freelancers have higher rates, so if you struggle to find someone to fill a role, seeking out newer or less experienced creatives may be the solution.

Contracts

I'll be the first to admit it, sending contracts to cast and crew can be intimidating. But they're really helpful. A contract between the showrunner and cast (or crew) member lays out the expectations of their exchange in writing. The expectation of the showrunner is usually receiving completed work for their show — a script, recorded lines, edited audio, etc. The expectation of the cast or crew member is usually receiving payment. A contract ensures both parties are in agreement on what they need to do and when. How long does a voice actor have to record once receiving the script? How long after getting the actor's audio before the showrunner pays them?

A contract should also make it clear who owns the work and how it will be used. For voice actors, this can be as easy as making sure you have permission to use their recordings in your show (this can be called a Talent Release Form). For writers, it can be trickier, as you should outline who owns the IP and can use it going forward.

For *Someone Dies In This Elevator*, an anthology show, writers owned their scripts. They were welcome to include it on their website or send it around without asking permission. If they wanted to create a spin-off of their story, even a spin off that was an audio drama, it was fine with me. Because *Someone Dies In This Elevator* was an anthology show, the writer of an episode also created the world that episode was set in *and* all the characters in it. If they wanted to have a character show up in another story, it was fine with me. *Someone Dies In This Elevator* only owned the final episode audio.

In *Sidequesting*, guest writers did not create the world. As a serialized show, the worldbuilding had already been established by me. Therefore, I didn't want writers creating a spin-off of their story because it would have been a spinoff of *Sidequesting*, my audio drama. However, when guest writers created new characters for the main character of the story to meet, they owned their characters. While they did not have the rights to Sidequesting as a whole (or the characters I created), writers could share their scripts without my permission.

These two examples illustrate how nitty-gritty you can get in contracts. When creating a contract, I recommend making your best guesses as to what people might want to do with their work down the line, and outline if it's acceptable or not.

In addition to establishing the scope of work, a contract should also establish what happens when either party breaks the agreement, such as a writer not turning in a script or a showrunner being late to pay an actor.

Many audio drama contracts also include a no-AI clause, informing voice actors or writers that their audio or scripts will not be used to train an AI to copy it. Some freelancers will not work with you if you plan to put their work through generative AI.

Contracts can also include a Nondisclosure Agreement clause, also called an NDA. This agreement prevents someone from sharing information, like scripts or audio, before it is publicly released.

Here is an audio drama contract template that you can use as a starting point for your show:

This template has not been created or reviewed by anyone in the legal profession. I recommend consulting with an attorney or legal expert if possible. I am not a lawyer, and this is not legal advice.

The following agreement is entered into as of [DATE] between the following parties: [YOUR NAME] (hereby referred to as "Client") and [CAST/CREW NAME] (hereby referred to as "Freelancer"), for the project known as [AUDIO DRAMA NAME] (hereby referred to as "Production").

Client's Obligations

Payment

- Client shall provide payment in full at the rate of [RATE] within 30 business days of receipt of work. Client shall compensate Freelancer for any assigned work completed, regardless of whether the work is ultimately used in Production.
- Payment provided after 30 business days of receipt of work shall accrue a late payment fee of 1.5% per week.
- Client shall compensate Freelancer for additional work requested beyond the scope of the initial agreements. Compensation shall be negotiated before additional work is started, and provided within 30 business days of receipt of work.

- Client shall keep confidential any personal information of Freelancer provided for the purposes of completing the job or receiving payment, except as legally necessary.

Scope of Work

- Client shall convey any necessary instructions to Freelancer upon or prior to beginning work. If information and files required to complete the services are not received within 2 weeks of the agreed deadline, the deadline shall be renegotiated.
- Client shall not require Freelancer to promote Production on social media or participate in other promotional activities unless a separate promotional agreement is entered into.
- Client may choose to use Freelancer's provided credit name and/or likeness to promote Production, so long as it is not done in a disparaging or misleading manner.
- [FOR VOICE ACTORS] Client acknowledges that the scope of work applies only to the raw voiceover recordings and does not include mixing, mastering, or other editing (beyond basic cleanup), unless arranged with Freelancer prior to recording.
- [FOR SCRIPT WRITERS] Client acknowledges that the scope of work applies only to the written script and does not include audio recording or production, unless arranged with Freelancer prior to writing.

- [FOR AUDIO EDITORS] Any audio assets used within the podcast shall be attributed to their rightful owners and used only after gaining the appropriate copyright licenses.

Credit

- Client will credit Freelancer on Production website, in the end credits audio of Production episodes which Freelancer worked on, and in the show notes of Production episodes which Freelancer worked on.

- Client will use the credit name as written at the end of this document.

Freelancer's Obligations

Scope of Work

- Freelancer shall perform work at the agreed-upon rate for the duration of Production installment.

- Freelancer shall, in good faith, perform quality work according to Client's direction and specifications. If a mistake is made on Freelancer's part, Freelancer shall fix the mistake at no extra charge to Client. If a mistake is made on Client's part, negotiation for additional payment may take place.
- Freelancer shall deliver work by the agreed-upon deadlines, excepting emergency circumstances. Should Freelancer become unable to perform the work as scheduled, Freelancer shall inform Client as soon as reasonably possible.

- Should Freelancer not deliver all work by the agreed-upon deadline, it shall be considered a termination of the agreement and any future work will be subject to a renegotiation. Freelancer is not entitled to compensation for portions of the work not completed.

- All deliverables will be a result of Freelancer's own work and artificially generated nor infringe on intellectual property rights.

- Freelancer shall keep confidential any personal information of Client provided for the purposes of completing the job or providing payment, except as legally necessary.

- [FOR VOICE ACTORS] One round of pickups requested during the audio editing process is included in the scope of work.

- [FOR VOICE ACTORS] Upon completion of the services and confirmation of receipt of deliverables, files will be stored by Freelancer for one month. Any requests by Client for copies of raw files or deliverables after this period may not be fulfilled.

- [FOR AUDIO EDITORS] Upon completion of the services and confirmation of receipt of deliverables, files will be stored by Freelancer for three months. Any requests by Client for copies of raw files or deliverables after this period may not be fulfilled.

Use and Ownership

- Freelancer is an Independent Contractor, not an employee, of Client. Client will not provide fringe benefits, including health insurance benefits, paid vacation, or any other employee benefit.

- Freelancer acknowledges the work as a "buyout" for the agreed rate and that Client is not obligated to provide any residuals, royalties, bonuses, or additional use fees.

- Nothing in this agreement obligates Client to use the work performed by Freelancer.

- Client shall not use Freelancer's work to train machine learning algorithms or distribute the assets for such purposes to third-party companies, without Freelancer's express and informed consent.

- Freelancer provides an irrevocable and perpetual license to Client to use, modify, publish and distribute the work for Production and all related materials, with the explicit exception of usage for artificial intelligence purposes.

- [FOR VOICE ACTORS] Freelancer is providing a "work made for hire" and retains no ownership, copyright, or moral rights claim to the recordings used in Production.

- [FOR VOICE ACTORS] Client will not create a synthetic reproduction of Freelancer's voice or otherwise simulate Freelancer's voice using artificial intelligence or text-to-speech programs (regardless of whether such simulated voice is identifiable as belonging to Freelancer).

- [FOR SCRIPT WRITERS] Client will not create a synthetic reproduction of Freelancer's writing or otherwise simulate Freelancer's writing using artificial intelligence programs (regardless of whether such simulated writing is identifiable as belonging to Freelancer).

- [FOR AUDIO EDITORS] By providing Freelancer with any audio or other media (collectively "Creator Content"), the client grants Freelancer the non-exclusive, worldwide right to use such Creator Content in association with their services and in their marketing, including self promotion and/or educational presentations.

Non-Disclosure Agreement

- Freelancer shall keep confidential any information regarding Production prior to official public release or announcement of Freelancer's work therein.

- Both Freelancer and Client understand that while sensitive and/or proprietary information may be exchanged in the course of work on Production, such information shall not be disclosed to unrelated parties, or publicly disseminated (including, but not limited to, in social media posts, blogs, interviews, or public appearances) without prior clearance.

- Shall Freelancer's willful disclosure of proprietary information cause irreparable damages to Client, Client reserves the right to seek legal action as deemed necessary.

Termination

- Both parties are entitled to terminate this agreement with immediate effect if the other party demonstrates purposeful oppressive or harmful actions against a marginalized or vulnerable societal group in the course of any and all part of their business.

- If either party desires to terminate this agreement for any other reason, notice must be provided in writing to the other party 2 weeks prior to the effective date of termination.

- If any provision of this agreement shall be held to be invalid or unenforceable for any reason, the remaining provisions shall continue to be valid and enforceable. If a court finds that any provision of this agreement is invalid or unenforceable, but that by limiting such provision it would become valid and enforceable, then such provision shall be deemed to be written, construed, and enforced as so limited.

- The failure of either party to enforce any provision of this agreement shall not be construed as a waiver or limitation of that party's right to subsequently enforce and compel strict compliance with every provision of this agreement.

Chapter 7

Recording

You have a script. You have your cast and crew. Time for the next step: sending a bunch of emails! Yeah, I know. It's not a fun task, but before you can get together to record, you've got to *schedule* getting together to record.

Before formally kicking off production, you should onboard your cast and crew so that everyone has an idea of how production will take place. Either collect your team online in a Slack or Discord server, create a production newsletter, or prepare to send a lot of individual emails. You'll probably have to do this last one regardless. Basically, no matter how you do it, communication is key.

Before you meet to record, your cast should have an idea of:

- The basic concept of the show, including episode and season length
- The tentative schedule for each step of production, from recording to audio editing to final mixing
- Who they can ask questions to
- Who they can report issues to

- What the rate of pay will be, and the expected hours of commitment
- How audio files should be formatted when sent in
- When they can announce their involvement in the show
- If they will be recording on their own or in live-directed sessions

You might be recording audio remotely (where each person is in a different room, on a different mic), or recording in person at a studio. Recording might be happening synchronously or asynchronously. Synchronous recording is when actors record together and play off each other's performances. It's like a table read — envision all the actors in a room or on a call together. Asynchronous recording is when actors record their parts separately. They're not acting with another actor.

Every production works slightly differently, so don't assume there is a standard that your voice actors abide by. It's important to communicate your plans and expectations. This is your responsibility as the showrunner, not the actors' responsibility to know what you're expecting them to do without being told.

Vocabulary Breakdown:

- **Remote Recording:** The actors record from a home studio.
- **In-Person Recording:** The actors travel to a location to record.

- **Live Recording:** An actor records live with a director (and usually other actors, but not always), either via a call or in person. Think of live recordings as something that must be scheduled by a producer or director.
- **Solo Recording:** An actor records on their own, without a director (or other actors) present. The actor is provided a deadline, sets their own time to record, and self-directs their session.
- **Synchronous Recording:** Actors record together on a call or in person (usually with a director). These sessions can be remote or in person, but they are always live.
- **Asynchronous Recording:** Actors record their parts separate from each other. A director may be present (making it a live session), but usually the actor is alone (making it a solo session).

The most common scenarios in indie audio drama are *remote solo asynchronous recording* (actors are given the script and record on their own), *remote live synchronous recording* (actors meet in a group call and record with each other and a director), and *in-person live synchronous recording* (actors travel to a studio and record with each other and a director). Because all synchronous recordings are also live recordings, the "live" part is usually dropped when it precedes "synchronous." Asynchronous recordings can be either live or solo; usually they are assumed to be solo unless specifically stated.

It's less common to have *live asynchronous recording* (directed sessions for a single voice actor at a time), but it's not unheard of. When schedules don't align, a common process is to record a scene with the available voice actors, and ask the others to record asynchronously (either in a live session with the director or fully solo). Shows with long monologues may also decide to do *live asynchronous recording* (with just a director and an actor) or *solo asynchronous recording* (the actor recording on their own), so that other actors aren't sitting through long swaths of an actor's performance, which is what would happen in a *synchronous recording* session.

You don't have to commit to one scenario for your whole show. You can pick some scenes for actors to record alone, and organize live/synchronous sessions for others. For *Re: Dracula*, we chose to have our director present for "high-impact" scenes, usually with emotional beats we wanted to nail. These were often group sessions (*live synchronous recording*), but occasionally it was just our director and an actor (*live asynchronous recording*). For the rest of the scenes, we had our actors record on their own time (*solo asynchronous recording*).

In Person Recording Tips:

If scheduling permits, get actors to record their scenes together so they can play off each other. Aim for synchronous recording when possible.

If the "studio" for your production is your own living room, I recommend doing your best to prevent reverb in the space (it will save you a headache later). Put down rugs or blankets. If there are any hard surfaces like glass tables, cover them up with a blanket as well. If you can, even put blankets or towels up on the walls.

If you're recording in a "real" studio, be sure to know if there will be a recording technician (if there isn't, surprise, the recording technician is now you!) and how audio will be sent to you. Ask what microphones they have and determine if multiple voice actors can record together. Some studios may be set up for a single person to record at a time.

Prevent crosstalk (actors talking over each other, or at the same time) if you're using mics that will pick up audio from a different part of the room.

If possible, use the same microphones for all the voice actors. Even if two people are in the same space, they can sound different if their mics aren't the same.

Remote Recording Tips:

For live sessions, you should record both sides of audio locally. If you're recording with a program like Zoom or Discord, don't rely on the quality of the recording from the program itself. Recording via Discord bot (or just recording your Zoom call) will give you worse audio quality. Each person recording on that call should also be recording locally to their own device, via Audacity or another DAW. If you have a director on hand, recording their vocal direction on its own track will be helpful for the dialogue editor down the road (more on that later).

For asynchronous sessions, ask for a few different takes. Ideally, each take will have a slightly different energy. This can be up to the actor to determine, or you can add direction in brackets before a line (such as "with a laugh" or "said angrily"). It's good practice to ask how your actors want direction. Some might prefer to get character information and then make their own calls on specific lines. Others might appreciate more detailed direction.

Regardless of how you do it, getting options for each line reading allows the dialogue editor to pick takes that flow well with each other. Sometimes there are also clicks or background noise an actor didn't catch in their recording, and asking for a second take in the initial asynchronous session can reduce the need to request retakes. In remote live sessions, it's not uncommon to record a final take "for safety" in case something is discovered to be wrong with a good take in the audio editing stage.

You should collect raw audio from your actors. This means audio with zero processing done to it: no noise reduction, no compressors, no filters, no fiddling with loudness or volume. Let your sound designer run noise reduction and do additional processing on the files. It's standard to collect files as a .wav format, though I avoid 16 bit .wav files because they often have noise that 24 bit .wav files do not. While .mp3 files take up less space, the audio is compressed and lower quality, so I avoid them as well.

Do not make your actors send in separate files for each line. This is called "line splitting," and it's a very tedious process. If your sound designer requests this, you should absolutely pay your voice actors for the additional work. It's not fair to request this work from volunteer voice actors. Ideally, you should adjust your audio editing process to work with larger files: either per scene or per episode, not per line. I've yet to find a good reason to use line splitting for audio drama. Line splitting is typically used in video games — and even then, with mixed results and much more work on your actors' shoulders.

Provide your actors with technical info so they know what file formats to send to you for their own recordings. In general, you should have a discussion with your audio editors before defining these requirements for actors. If you're the audio editor and new to the task, you should do some test edits to figure out what works best for you.

Here's the technical info I've sent to voice actors for asynchronous recording:

1. 2–3 takes of each line, all in one file, AABBCC format
2. Name your files EpisodeNumber_CharacterName
3. 24 bit .wav file
4. Audio in mono preferred (but stereo is acceptable)
5. Include 10 seconds of room tone at the end of your recording
6. State the name you'd like to be credited with at the beginning

Additional notes on this technical info:

1. AABBCC format means I like to have multiple takes of one line before moving to the next one. ABCABC would be to record the entire script, and then start from the top once you've done it. Some people

prefer this in their editing process, and it makes more sense to do when recording live.

2. This file name works when actors are recording whole episodes at a time. You might need to request file names including page or scene numbers if episodes aren't being recorded in full.
3. I wanted 24 bit .wav files because 32 bit .wav files take up a lot of storage space.
4. I prefer mono audio because it takes up less storage space. I also don't want voice actor audio moving from one ear to another without the sound designer doing it. When I get stereo audio from actors, I turn it into mono. This is only a little extra work in Audition or Audacity, so I don't mind doing it if an actor forgets or is unsure how. It's a more complicated process in Pro Tools, so if I were using that DAW, I might be less forgiving.
5. Some noise reduction programs require a sample of room tone (the sound of the room with nobody speaking) in order to work. It's worth checking with your sound designer if this is something they want. If you're the sound designer, look into your audio editing program and decide before recording starts.
6. I want to be triple sure I say an actor's name correctly in the credits. For instances where I am only getting one file, I'll include this bullet point in the technical info. For instances where I'm getting multiple files, I'll usually request name pronunciation separately.

Other Recording Tips:

Get actors' permission before pitch shifting or otherwise altering their voice. It is really jarring as a voice actor to listen to a final episode and hear your voice has been surprisingly altered. It is especially uncomfortable for trans and non-binary voice actors to hear their voice unexpectedly pitched up or down. For some roles, like fantasy monsters, pitch shifting may be expected. You can include this information on your casting call instead of contacting the actor after recording if you're planning to do voice altering.

It is useful to have a place where voice actors can submit their files. I prefer to use a Google Drive folder or a Dropbox folder. It's annoying to send files via email, especially large ones, given most email clients' attachment size limits. Google Drive will often use the uploader's personal storage to host the file, so if you're collecting large amounts of audio with it, it will be helpful for your voice actors if you're able to download them locally and then delete the file from Google Drive.

For audio dramas with lots of scenes and lots of characters, file management becomes a task on its own. As producer, it will be your job to make sure all the audio has been recorded. It can be useful to create a spreadsheet of each character in each episode, and mark it off when you've collected the audio. Such a spreadsheet can also come in handy when scheduling recording sessions by allowing you to know, at a quick glance, which voice actors are in what scene. This can be done using Google Sheets, or products like Airtable, Notion, or Asana for more robust features.

Acting and Directing

A lot of indie showrunners find themselves acting in or directing their own productions, often with little prior experience. I'm not here to teach you the specifics of becoming an actor or director, but here's some general advice.

For more in-depth learning, check out *Acting: The First Six Lessons* by Richard Boleslavsky, and *Directing Actors* by Judith Weston.

Acting

Get used to the sound of your own voice. Most people hate it when they start out, but the best way to improve your acting is to listen back to it. Evaluate your performance with a critical edge. What could you have done better? Don't be afraid to take on new angles or try weird things in the booth. It very well could sound different listening back.

Don't forget to warm up your voice before recording. This can be done with formal exercises, or it can be as simple as singing in your apartment before entering the booth. I'll confess to sometimes doing auditions for other shows as a warm-up. Do whatever works for you!

There is a surprising amount of physicality in voice acting. I record standing up, and I wiggle all over the place. I've ruined takes by bumping the mic with all my gestures. Your recording space may be cramped, but if you have the option to move while recording, try it out. Match what the character is doing. If they're jumping, jump! If they're lifting, lift! If you don't have the option to move your body, move your face.

Smile, frown, stick up your nose . . . it will make the lines sound different than if you were sitting down and staying still.

Unlike theater, voice acting doesn't need to be big. You're not projecting your voice for the back of the audience — you're speaking into a microphone right next to you. Audio drama as a medium is perfect for lower key, more intimate performances. You can literally whisper in the audience's ear. Take advantage of that! This isn't to say there's no such thing as big, dramatic characters in audio drama. You'll have your chances to go ham, but don't feel pressured to make every character over the top. Get a feel for the style of voice acting used in audio dramas by listening to other shows. This also varies by genre!

Finding the right microphone to use could be a book all on its own . . . a book that would very quickly be out of date. My advice is to ask other creators what mics they're using and why they like it. In general, an XLR mic will sound better than a USB mic. But there are good and bad options for both; purchasing an XLR mic does not put you "in the clear." Different mics will sound good on different voice types (in fact, this might be a reason to *not* have all your actors on the same mic for in person recording).

Creating the right recording space is just as important as finding the right microphone, if not more. Unfortunately, it's frequently overlooked. You should treat the space you're recording in to remove both background noise and echoes. This can be as simple as turning the AC off while recording, or as complicated as building a blanket fort to sit in. Before I converted a walk-in closet to a home studio, I recorded facing an open closet in my bedroom so that my clothes would dampen reverb. I'd put blankets and pillows over my furniture for better acoustics. It was certainly a process, but it made a clear difference. Before recording final audio for your audio drama, do some test recordings with different room treatments and see what sounds best.

Directing

Avoid reading a line how you want the actor to perform it. It's generally frowned upon. Line reading as a director removes the freedom of interpretation for an actor and harms the collaborative spirit of a director-actor relationship. It also shows you don't trust the actor to receive directorial feedback, or that you don't trust yourself to give it. Instead, try to vocalize what you want from that performance. Here are some examples:

- "Keep the same amount of anger, but try being quieter."
- "Can you give me this line like it's the worst thing you've had to say?"
- "Do you think the character would sound more exhausted after all this running?"
- "Try reading this line with your teeth clenched."
- "Give me 50% less energy in this take."
- "Mimic lifting a heavy box for this part."

When there isn't a table read, utilize the first run through of the script as a warm-up. I like to record the first take in case it results in something great, but usually I find myself pulling later takes for the show audio. I'll tend to do 3 takes total: 1 for warmup, 1 for "the real deal," and 1 for safety. Sometimes when I'm directing, I'll tell my actors to take it farther for the final take instead of just doing a backup take for safety. I've found it gives more options (and better acting) than actors trying to repeat what they did in their previous take. Past 3 full takes, If I want additional takes of a section, I'll go back to just that section (or the specific lines) instead of doing a fourth recording of the entire episode.

Three run-throughs of the script may be too many if it's a long episode. It's important to keep sessions short, because energy will flag after the first hour or two. At times, it may be necessary to redo a short section of the script instead of the entire scene to get an alternate take. Don't shy away from that option, especially if you're recording a long episode.

In the same vein, avoid unnecessary chit-chat at the start of a recording session. A little discussion to break the ice can be great, but it shouldn't run more than a few minutes. Save talk unrelated to the recording session for the end of it, so that it doesn't run late and people can leave if they want to.

Voice Actor Incidentals

Incidental audio is all those little moments of sound people make that aren't quite words. A deep breath. An exasperated sigh. A grunt. A whimper. Adding sounds like these throughout your production will make your characters seem more real and the story seem more believable. These are also known as "effort sounds."

You can create a list of incidentals based on your specific story, or you can collect a more general set from your actors to hand to the sound designer. Sound designers will be very happy to have these extra sounds to heighten moments. Sometimes I ask for these incidentals separately, but other times I work them into the script.

You might ask for a separate list for fight or chase scenes, where having a myriad of different sounds to use in conjunction with SFX is beneficial. But if you only need a handful of sounds, having a call-out in the script will provide specific context to the voice actor, and may be easier to coordinate.

Some examples of specific incidentals:

- Measured, heavy breathing for a scene where a character is running
- Exertion sounds of hitting/throwing/swinging a weapon (if you have a fight scene, get a lot of these)
- Reactions to being hurt/injured (if you have a fight scene, get a lot of these as well)
- A sound for lifting something heavy
- A sound for landing a jump
- Humming for a scene where a character is doing a mundane task
- Tense breathing for a scene where a character is hiding
- Shivering for a scene set in the cold

- If a character is crying during a scene, additional sniffling/crying for when they're not talking
- If a character is sick, additional sniffling/coughing for when they're not talking

Other general incidentals include:

- A quick huff of irritation
- A slow sigh, a deep breath
- A thoughtful, "Hmmmm …"
- A confused, "Uhhh...?"
- A small laugh/chuckle
- A big, authentic laugh
- A small cough or clearing of the throat

You'll know your script better than anyone else, and you should be able to make the call as to what sort of incidentals would fit in the script. In the writing stage, it can be hard to think about what's happening while characters are talking. In the sound design stage, it's all you're thinking about. Collecting a list of incidentals will save sound designer–you from cursing writer-you. Or, if you're hiring a sound designer, they'll think you're really cool.

Chapter 8

Audio Editing

Audio Editing can mean many different things, but they all take place in a DAW, or Digital Audio Workstation. Think Audacity, Reaper, Adobe Audition, Garageband, Logic, etc. I used Audacity myself until the limitations of the program hindered what I wanted to do, and then I moved to Audition.

There's a lot of bickering about DAWs in the podcasting sphere. You're going to hear all sorts of things about which is best, why you shouldn't be using a particular DAW, why you should feel bad for using or not using any specific DAW. Frankly, I think you should just find what works for you and go with it. Do your research on the pros and cons of each option and just pick one. In general, the best DAW is the one you know how to use. If the one you're using starts getting in your way, learn another.

If you want to start with something simple and easy to learn, I recommend Audacity or Garageband. If you want something more versatile, check out Reaper, Logic, or Audition. There are more DAWs than I've mentioned here (like Pro Tools, Cubase, FL Studio, and Ableton), and each has their strengths and weaknesses.

The jobs that are done with a DAW are frequently bundled into one category of "audio editing" or "audio production," but if you're hiring someone, make sure the two of you are on the same page about their job duties. Are they picking takes? Editing dialogue? Doing sound design? Mastering the audio? It can all blur together, so discussing specific definitions can be helpful. Here's a vocabulary breakdown for different parts of the process.

Picking Takes: Taking the raw recording from the actors and deciding which take to choose when multiple were recorded. This is often the director's job, but it sometimes goes to the dialogue editor or showrunner (if those people are distinct from the director). Sometimes this involves opening a DAW and deleting the takes you don't want; other times, it involves listening through each take and providing your dialogue editor with written instructions of which take to use. This latter situation is often used for more general instructions like, "Go with the second take of this scene." Avoid writing out detailed per-line instructions if you can. At that point, you'd be better off deleting the takes yourself in a DAW.

Dialogue Editing: Taking the selected takes and ordering them according to the script. The biggest thing a dialogue editor does is decide timing, which is especially relevant for asynchronous recordings. However, timing takes properly is an art, no matter the format of the recording session. I've noticed that the dialogue edits I do on live-but-remotely-recorded sessions involve tightening the dialogue by removing lag from the call. Good dialogue editing will make a conversation feel real. The best way to practice dialogue editing timing is to listen to more conversations. Pay attention to the timing of dialogue in movies and films, and of course, other audio dramas. Try to channel the characters' personalities and emotional states when considering timing. If the character is excited, do they speak faster? If they're annoyed, would they cut someone off, or make someone wait for every response?

Sound Design: Taking the dialogue edit and building the audio world around it. There is action sound design (adding SFX for what the characters are doing) and environmental sound design (adding SFX to represent the environment). Sound designers may do their own scoring, or work with the show's composer to incorporate their music into each scene. Sometimes a sound designer will record their own sound effects, and other times they'll pull from their own collection of royalty-free SFX.

Mixing and Mastering: Cleaning and leveling the dialogue, music, and SFX. Often the sound designer is in charge of this too. It's making all the final tweaks, so the episode sounds the best it possibly can.

Here's an example:

[SFX] BOATSWAIN stands on a ship at sea: a tempestuous noise. *Enter ALONSO and ANTONIO.*

1. *ALONSO: Good boatswain, have care. Where's the master? Play the men.*
2. *BOATSWAIN: I pray now, keep below.*
3. *ANTONIO: Where is the master, boatswain?*
4. *BOATSWAIN: Do you not hear him? You mar our labour: keep your cabins: you do assist the storm.*

We've got three actors for four lines. I will call the actors by their character names: Alonso, Boatswain, and Antonio. Let's say these actors recorded three takes of each line. I've labeled each take A, B and C (i.e. The first take of line 1 will be labeled 1A, the third take of line 2 will be labeled 2)

Alonso: 1A, 1B, 1C

Boatswain: 2A, 2B, 2C, 4A, 4B, 4C

Antoni: 3A, 3B, 3C

The person picking takes will listen though and decide which one to go with. Let's say our director has chosen 1C, 2A, 4A, and 3B. The dialogue editor will take these four lines and order/time them appropriately (1C, 2A, 3B, and 4A). We now have the full exchange in audio.

The sound designer will take the clip of this exchange and add sound effects. For our action SFX, we've got characters walking in the beginning. The sound designer would probably add two pairs of footsteps on wood to reflect this. For our environmental SFX, we've got the sound of a ship in a storm. The sound designer would probably add the sounds of waves crashing, a ship rocking, thunder, lightning, rain, etc. They may also apply filters to the audio of these actors to better reflect their environment.

Occasionally, the sound designer will pass their audio off to someone else to master it. For example, they might ensure the episode meets an industry standard loudness level. This person makes everything sound its best, and produces the final product.

Dialogue Editing Details

Often the dialogue editor is also picking takes, especially when they're the showrunner. Take selection is relatively easy for synchronous recording, when actors are playing off each other. It's a matter of listening through the scenes and finding the exchanges you like best. Sometimes a dialogue editor may combine their favorite sentences from separate takes. When clips from two takes are used for different parts of the same line, it's often referred to (lovingly) as a "frankenline."

I'll use lowercase to demonstrate take 1, and uppercase to demonstrate take 2.

Take 1: i can't wait to go to the store and get, uh green apples?
Take 2: I CANNOT WAIT TO GET TO MY STORE AND BUY RED APPLES.

Frankenline: i can't wait to go to the store AND BUY RED APPLES.

The beginning of the line is from the first take and the end of the line is from the second take. The takes will have to have been similar in tone and volume for a listener to not notice the cut between them.

In asynchronous recordings, dialogue editing becomes more difficult because you have to put exchanges together before you listen to them in full. Picking takes out of context is difficult; not only do you have to keep directorial goals in your head and remember what alternate takes of the scene sounded like, you also have to remember what the other actors in the scene were doing. Good dialogue editing can mask asynchronous recording by picking voice actor takes that complement each other, making it seem like the actors were recorded in the same room at the same time.

In synchronously recorded scenes, most of my dialogue editing is specific timing adjustments once takes have been decided. Remote recording can introduce longer pauses between exchanges, and I prefer to make conversations snappier in the edit. Once minor flubs are removed (such as someone saying the wrong word and re-doing a line), I'm mostly tightening back and forth exchanges. This even happens for in-person sessions, sometimes. In real life, people tend to talk over each other, running on top of the ends of sentences. This happens less often for actors reading off a script. As a dialogue editor, my goal is usually to make conversations more realistic, so I manually adjust the timing to simulate cross talk and characters interrupting each other.

For asynchronous scenes, I will pick takes as I dialogue edit. This is why I usually ask for an AABBCC take style. Let's say we have the exchange from the previous example:

1. *ALONSO: Good boatswain, have care. Where's the master? Play the men.*
2. *BOATSWAIN: I pray now, keep below.*
3. *ANTONIO: Where is the master, boatswain?*
4. *BOATSWAIN: Do you not hear him? You mar our labour: keep your cabins: you do assist the storm.*

Pretending this short exchange is an entire scene, I would have three files: Alonso, Boatswain, and Antonio. Alonso and Antonio's files would be the one line, and Boatswain would have two lines. Asking for three takes would yield audio like this. I'll put each take in brackets.

Alonso: [Good boatswain, have care. Where's the master? Play the men.] [Good boatswain, have care. Where's the master? Play the men.] [Good boatswain, have care. Where's the master? Play the men.]

Botswain: [I pray now, keep below.] [I pray now, keep below.] [I pray now, keep below.] [Do you not hear him? You mar our labour: keep your cabins: you do assist the storm.] [Do you not hear him? You mar our labour: keep your cabins: you do assist the storm.] [Do you not hear him? You mar our labour: keep your cabins: you do assist the storm.]

Antonio: [Where is the master, boatswain?] [Where is the master, boatswain?] [Where is the master, boatswain?]

You can see why I wrote it out like "Alonso: 1A, 1B, 1C; Boatswain: 2A, 2B, 2C, 4A, 4B, 4C; Antonio: 3A, 3B, 3C" before!

Now, I could listen to these takes in the order written out and pick my favorite from each of them. However, what if the energy of the takes were something like:

Alonso: (extremely worried)[1A] (generally concerned)[1B] (near whisper)[1C]

Botswain: (pleading)[2A] (reprimanding)[2B] (neutral), (reprimanding)[4A] (shouting)[4B] (exasperated)[4C]

Antonio: (shouting)[3A] (extremely worried)[3B] (very scared)[3C]

Maybe out of context, Alonso's near whisper line is best and Antonio's shouting line is best. But paired together in the scene, they'll have very different energies. Maybe you think it makes sense for the characters to be loud during this storm. You'd probably pick 1A or 1B for Alonso and 3A for Antonio. Following that train of thought, 2B and 4A or 4B might make sense for the Botswain. Perhaps you want to go with a quieter, tenser scene. You'd maybe pick 1C for Alonso, 3C for Antonio, and 2A and 4A for Botswain.

Dialogue editing for asynchronous recording sessions is a powerful tool! Knowing the context of the scene and your options for performances before picking final takes will elevate your dialogue edit. A bad dialogue edit will make character chemistry feel off and prevent performances from truly meshing. A good dialogue edit will slip unnoticed into the background, and the audio drama will feel more real because of it.

In a dialogue edit, each character should be on their own track in the DAW. If your DAW can't handle multiple tracks, this is a good reason to seek out a different one. Putting characters on separate tracks will allow the sound designer to not only better control timing, but also add filters to each character, track by track. For example, one voice actor may need more noise reduction on their files than another. Having two tracks for each of these voice actors means that noise reduction can be run on the entire track, instead of manually picking and choosing which clips to edit.

Usually, dialogue editors are not expected to process actor audio. If your dialogue editor is different from your sound designer, make sure both individuals are on the same page about this. It might make sense for the dialogue editor to run noise reduction and level the audio, or your sound designer may want to do that themself. If you're doing both roles yourself, you get to decide when you take care of each step of the process!

Sound Design Details

I could go on forever and ever about sound design. It's my favorite part of the process. I love that sound design is as simple or detailed as you want to make it. Instead of going deep into the technical nature of it, I'll be focusing on the thought process behind bringing a scene to life.

Most sound design can be broken into "environmental" and "action" sound design. Vocals and music are also part of the process, though with the help of dialogue editors and composers they can be easier to manage.

A "soundscape" is everything a listener hears. It usually creates a sense of immersion and sells the scene. In a novel, you have descriptive paragraphs. In an audio drama, you have the soundscape.

A soundscape consists of:

- Environment
    - Background Noise
    - Echo/Reverb
    - Room tone
- Actions
    - Footsteps

    - Panning
    - Items
- Voices
- Music

When building a scene, you should ask yourself these questions:

Where is this taking place? Is the room empty? What details of the room are important for the audience to know? Are the walls hard or soft? What is the floor made of?

Where are the people and objects placed in the space of the scene? How many are there? How does the audience know they're there?

What are those people and objects doing in the scene? What does that sound like? Is there diegetic background music, like at a modern restaurant?

You might take a note that reads, "A stone cave with a wooden platform hanging from rope. Two characters enter the cave, then go on the platform," and break it down like so:

- Ambience: Cave Drone
- Reverb: Big Echo
- Footsteps: Gravel, then creaky wood
- Panning: Characters 15L and 15R
    - This means one of the characters will be panned 15% to the right speaker, and the

other character will be panned 15% to the left speaker.

- Items: Stone door, flashlight, hanging platform (wood and ropes)
- Music: Foreboding, blending with cave

Here's another example: "INT. Warehouse. SFX: Suri passes a somewhat heavy canister to Jules. Jules opens it and dumps it on the ground in front of them."

- Ambience: Warehouse (large)
- Reverb: Yes
- Footsteps: Tile
- Panning: Not in this scene
- Items: Canister and liquid
- Music: None

But this scene comes with additional decisions. What does the canister sound like being picked up, passed over, opened, poured, and set down? How does the liquid hit the ground? Is it being poured in one place or splashed over a larger area? That's what is tricky about action SFX. It needs to be broken up into each step containing a specific sound.

Acquiring SFX

You've got a lot of options for acquiring SFX to use in your audio drama. A simple search will lead you to sites like Asoundeffect selling royalty-free sounds or sites like Freesound with free-to-use SFX. There are also websites that offer access to their entire catalog for a monthly fee, reducing the need to buy specific sound packs.

Don't go around ripping sound effects from just anywhere, because you're likely violating copyright. It's important to understand the terms and conditions for sounds you download. Freesound, for example, is a database of user uploads. Some sounds are public domain, others require attributions (credit to whoever made the sound), and others require attribution and are made for non-commercial projects only.

If you want to monetize your audio drama, avoid using non-commercial copyright SFX. Some websites, like Zapsplat, require attribution if you download effects for free, but not if you pay per sound or subscribe to their monthly plan. Any sound packs you download from sites like Asoundeffect should come with a document that lays out the legal details for their use.

If you plan to sound design audio dramas in a variety of different genres, a subscription plan (like the one offered by Epidemic Sound) may be the better route. If you're working mostly in one style and can cover your bases with a handful of packs, you probably don't need a subscription.

My show *Sidequesting* is "a fantasy podcast about avoiding the main plot." I leaned heavily on a pack of forest sounds, a pack of outdoor footsteps, a pack of medieval town noises, and a handful of additional sword SFX. I supplemented my sound design with occasional audio from Freesound and recording my own sounds. This worked great for me! I ended up using several sounds I bought for *Sidequesting* for other audio dramas too. It was nice to have them on hand indefinitely in my hard drive.

Recording your own sound effects, also called foley work, is really fun, and it's a useful tool for cheap SFX. Many times have I worked on Slice of Life shows and recorded clips around my apartment to use in the sound design. Examples included: hugging, slamming a cupboard, handling silverware, setting a plate down, clinking mugs, checking a pocket for a wallet, rolling dice. In these Slice of Life shows, I found myself in situations requiring specific sounds that weren't widely available. It was truly faster to bring my mic to the kitchen and get the right sounds instead of digging around online for something I could finagle into place.

Handheld recorders are best for recording sound effects, because you don't need to lug a laptop around nor deal with the sound of its fans. You should try to record one sound at a time, such as a fan whirring OR a cat meowing, not both at once. This is because it's easy to layer the sounds in post, but difficult to separate them.

If you're recording an ambient environment, such as a museum gallery, this matters less. For environmental recording, it's best to avoid distinct conversations; try to place your recorder away from most foot traffic, in a remote place where the voices mingle and blur. If you're in a place that requires two-party consent for recordings, be sure to familiarize yourself with your local laws about recording environmental audio in public.

Environmental Sound Design

The name of the game here is room tone, which is the sound of the room your characters are in. It's important to have something to set the environment, even when your characters are somewhere quiet. No place is fully quiet. Even sitting in your living room, you're likely to hear appliances running and muffled sounds outside the room, coming in through walls or windows. That's room tone. A great exercise is to sit somewhere, try to break down what you're hearing, and think about how you might replicate it.

In interior environments, creating a layer of ambience for the room is a crucial part of making all the characters sound like they're in the same space together. It's subtle, yes, but it goes a long way. I recommend purchasing a pack of interior ambiance or recording your bedroom for five minutes. Stick that SFX on any standard indoor scene, and you've got a great starting place.

In exterior environments, having a layer of ambience is crucial for setting the scene. It replaces the establishing shot in film and television. This also means that you don't need to have an "establishing shot" at the beginning of your scene: don't wait a few seconds to start the dialogue just so the audience can hear the room. They'll take it in under the dialogue.

However, listeners should never struggle to hear the dialogue because of the environment. It's okay to lower the volume of your busy street, have a blaring alarm shut down early, or slowly fade out a loud rushing stream. One of the key challenges in sound ensign is balancing realism with clarity. It's okay if your scene is a little less true to life if it prevents your audience from being confused. You can play with this balance, especially in situations where you want dialogue to be obscured. Think of the gag where a car drives by and honks to drown out a swear.

Action Sound Design

This type of sound design depicts what's happening in a scene. Often, things don't sound exactly as we think they do. For example, swords rarely whoosh when they swing, but sometimes it's more important to show that a sword has been swung than cling to how it would actually sound. We explored the limits of sound design in the "writing for sound" section; if you've done your job right in that stage, you should have an easier time now.

Another way I "cheat" sound design is by leaning into the emotions of a sound. If someone is sneaking on a wooden floor, you can bet that floor is way squeakier than it should be, because I want the scene to be tense. If someone is in an elevator that's malfunctioning, you bet I'm sticking metal grinding sounds in the scene that no elevator has actually made. Hugs are unnaturally loud because I want a listener to feel it. Chewing is unnaturally quiet, if present at all, because I don't want anyone to be grossed out. Once I stopped caring about how things *really* sound, and started caring about how I *wanted* them to sound, my sound work improved. The key to this is that sound design can *feel* real even if it doesn't exactly match the real world.

Layering is your best friend in action sound design. Usually, multiple things are happening at once in a scene. A moment with a sword swing might have the sound of cloth or armor moving, a step occurring alongside it, and then be followed up with a hit (and perhaps armor movement and steps from the opponent). If you want to emphasize that this was a strong hit, you might add a punchier impact sound than the higher pitched "sword hit armor" noise. The more layers you utilize, the more depth your sound design will have — to a point. It's certainly possible to go overboard, adding too many sounds on top of each other to the point where it all just sounds sort of muddy.

I have a few sound packs I keep coming back to for action sound design. They are a collection of cloth movements, a collection of bodyfalls, and a collection of footstep tracks. These sounds always elevate my scenes. The footsteps are my lazy way of having people walk indoors. I have tracks for running and walking, and a handful of different shoes. When I need to show someone is on the move, I drag in a track. Simple and easy. You can get really specific with footsteps, using specific footstep plugins and software, and it absolutely has its time and place . . . but a lot of the time, I just want the listener to know there is movement.

The cloth and bodyfall sound packs serve a different purpose. I'm constantly using them to elevate scenes in conjunction with different SFX. Cloth rustling is a very subtle sound, easy to forego without missing it. But when you add it to a scene, you get much more dimension. You hear characters move and interact, shift uncomfortably or relax. Bodyfall sounds serve a similar purpose. Whenever I need something to have more thump, I'm pulling from this pack. A flop on the couch. A punch to the gut. A jump from a ledge. Layering one (if not more) bodyfall sounds makes everything more visceral.

You might find different sounds or sound packs that you keep coming back to. Everyone is different! There are also absolutely different styles of sound design. Some people work hard to make their soundscapes as realistic as possible. Others focus only on the important sounds to the story. Some sound design takes on a dreamier feel, with sounds that wouldn't necessarily be present in real life. Other sound design leans into the weird and experimental. You'll find your style as you gain experience. You'll learn how style meshes with genre, what's important to a slice of life audio drama versus a sci-fi audio drama. Sound design is a deep well with endless possibilities, so play in the space!

Enhance Your Audio

This section is as technical as we're going to get. But it's not meant to be a crash course in sound design, it's meant to be a jumping-off point into further research and experimentation. Your homework is to explore.

Reverb is an incredible tool for setting an environment. No large, empty room is going to feel large and empty without voices echoing within. Reverb is also a great tool for making characters recorded in different places sound like they're in the same one. Even for scenes set in bedrooms or offices, I'm adding a touch of reverb if only to make the cast sound more cohesive. You don't need to start with anything fancy or expensive. Find one reverb plugin that gives you some sliders and dive in. Many DAWs even come with reverb tools and settings already built in, but your mileage may vary on their availability and their quality.

Panning is another great tool for setting an environment. With panning, you can move sounds from left to right on the sound output. Something panned 100% to the left would only come out of the left side speaker, headphone, or earbud. Something panned 50% to the left would have sound coming out of both speakers, but it would be louder on the left side, making the listener feel like the sound is coming from their left. The center sound output, with no panning, has both left and right speakers at the same volume and no directionality to the sound.

In most audio editing programs, you can pan an entire track or adjust individual clips. When working with multi-character scenes, I use panning as an extra tool to differentiate characters. Say there are five characters in a scene. The tracks will be spread out: 10R (10% to the right), 5R (5% to the right), 0 (no panning), 5L (5% to the left), 10L (10% to the left) . . . all fairly close to the center, but enough for a brain to notice and track in the background.

An important note regarding panning: avoid setting tracks all the way to one side. People with varied levels of hearing will listen to your production, including those who are hard of hearing in just one ear. Some people also choose to listen to podcasts with only one earbud. Don't make them miss out on half the dialogue!

Other times, I use panning to build movement into a scene. If people are coming and going from a room, I like to have the door panned left or right and fade the pan in and out as people use it. You can make things more complicated with panning by introducing binaural audio, or using plugins that simulate a 3D environment. These are advanced techniques, so be sure to look up specific guides before starting or expect a steep learning curve for figuring it out yourself.

There are an ever-growing number of plugins for audio editing. You do not need most of them. I recommend starting small and branching out bit by bit. A good starting place is to get a reverb plugin, as mentioned, and a noise reduction or audio mastering plugin. With these, you can go far. I use

PhoenixVerb and Izotope RX10 in nearly every project. I also get decent use out of a panning plugin and a voice modification plugin called LittleAlterBoy. But that's basically it. It's not worth spending big bucks on expensive software right out of the gate, especially when you're not sure what sorts of things you'll need to do.

The final technical note I have is about headphones. It's worth investing in a decent pair of wired headphones. Wireless headphones are always going to lose some audio quality, and they tend to have strange latency issues. This is another aspect you'll have to do your own research on, but I can guarantee the cheapest option will not be good enough. You will be determining the sound of your own show through this device, and if you listen through crappy earbuds while working, your final mix will suffer for it. However, don't throw those earbuds out just yet.

Is your sound design clear when listened via a subpar device? It's important to know the answer. Try the Car Speaker Test, in which you listen to your episode while driving, or the Crappy Earbuds Test, in which you listen on the cheapest pair of earbuds you can acquire. This mimics how part of the audience may be listening to your audio drama. What's clear on great headphones might not come across during rush hour or on a morning jog.

Music and Score

Many audio dramas don't utilize a score. They have a music track for the credits (and maybe the intro), and that's it. This is perfectly acceptable! You can also choose to only use music in important scenes, only under narration, or throughout the whole production. There's no one right answer for music in audio drama.

Like with royalty-free sound effects, there are royalty-free music tracks you can use in your production. Some of these are free, others are paid; some require attribution, others do not. Ensure you know the copyright information of music tracks before you include them in your audio drama. The last thing you want is a cease and desist letter.

You can also work with a composer to create original music for your audio drama, or learn the art of music making yourself. When working with a composer, it's important to be clear about what you want. Include the length of tracks and the mood you want to elicit. Linking examples of music you'd like to emulate or draw from can be a useful reference as well.

When adding music, make sure it doesn't drown out the vocals or SFX.

Shows with only intro/outro music:

- *What Will Be Here?*
- *Joy to the World*
- *Wanderer's Journal*
- *Inn Between*

Shows with royalty-free music:

- *Sidequesting*
- *Shelterwood*
- *NIGHTLIGHT*

- *Of The Sword*

Shows with original scoring:

- *Tales of the Echowood*
- *Re: Carmilla*
- *The Grotto*
- *Camlann*

Audio editing is the most critical part of audio drama production. It's what brings your story to life *in audio.* The best way to get better at dialogue editing and sound design is to practice. The second-best way is to listen to other audio dramas with a critical ear.

Tune in to other shows and find what aspects of their sound production you like. What makes the characters and scenes feel real? What's fun to listen to? Conversely, what takes you out of the show? What makes it difficult to suspend your disbelief?

Audio editing can be intimidating when you first jump in. It certainly was for me! But once I found out what worked for me, I learned it was incredibly fun to do. I hope you have a similar discovery!

Chapter 9

Finishing Touches

Once you've finished recording and producing your audio drama, you're *maybe* halfway done. It comes as a surprise to many first time creators, but there's an entire aspect to audio drama beyond the audio itself.

Show Title

I cannot over-stress the importance of a good title and cover art for your audio drama. It's the first thing people see when scrolling through a podcast app, the main thing people associate with your show, and can determine your level of success.

I recommend avoiding titles that are overly long or overly simplified. Some bad examples are: *"John's Big Adventure in New York City," "A Crisis of Big Proportions All Unexpected," "The Day I Found a Really Cool Rock in the Stream but it was CURSED,"* or on the other side of the spectrum, *"Tall," "Foolish" "The Man" "Sky" "Table"*. Be prepared to type your audio drama title out *a lot*.

Make sure your audio drama title has good SEO (Search Engine Optimization). Type your planned title into your search engine. What comes up? If there's already a famous book or movie with that name, you're setting yourself up to be hidden in search results. If there's already another podcast with that name, you're setting yourself up for marketing competition. If there's another *audio drama* with that name, you're setting yourself up for legal action.

Ideally, if someone searches up your audio drama, they should see it on the first page. At minimum, if they search "[Your Show Title] audio drama" or "[Your Show Title] podcast" they *really* should see it on the first page. As an example, my SEO is great for *What Will Be Here?* and *Re: Dracula,* but not so good for *Joy to the World* and *Falling Forward*. Surprisingly, a search for "Hubris Podcast" usually brings up "*Hubris: a 24 Hour Podcast Project*." The term "Sidequest" has become more popular since I coined *Sidequesting* in 2019, but the audio drama is still on the front page when you search "Sidequesting."

Cover Art

You want to capture the "vibes" of your audio drama with the art. Think of it like a book cover: your cover art should appeal to your target audience. We'll be getting more into the brand identity of your podcast in the marketing section; for now, you should know that your cover art is key to that brand. I recommend searching out other fiction podcasts in your genre and perusing their cover art. What shows stand out? What appeals to you? If you want to stand out (I recommend it!), do something different from what already exists.

Your cover art should be eye-catching but not too busy. All the elements of your art should be cohesive and go together. Don't feel pressured to include things that are present in your show (such as "my show heavily features a bedsheet ghost, so I will put a bedsheet ghost on the cover art"). You can get artsy or figurative with it. Lean into how your show *feels*.

This also means that you absolutely do not need headphones, a microphone, or sound waves on your cover art. You probably don't need a radio tower, record player, or cassette either. I promise your audience will know they're listening to a podcast without you saying THIS IS A PODCAST on your cover art. Movie posters don't usually have cameras or reels of film on them.

It's usually a good idea to include the title on it (ideally in a legible font), but avoid having too many words. You don't need to put who makes the show or who stars in it. This tends to be more of a problem with non-fiction podcasts than audio dramas, but you also don't need to put your face on your cover art.

It will come in handy to have a version of your cover art with no text, and a transparent png of just the text. These are useful for making additional promotional graphics.

I would gently discourage you from using AI-generated images for your cover art (as well as any other marketing materials). GenAI art has a specific, generic look to it. You're not going to end up with anything that stands out. It also sends the message that you don't value cover art enough to get a human to make it. AI is useful as a tool (for example, removing the background of an image), but it's lackluster when you depend on it for all your creativity.

Website

Your audio drama needs a website. Social media does not count. A default page generated by your podcast host does not count. Having a website will help people find your show and recommend it. It's the central place the audience can link to when talking about your work, and it's good to have everything about your audio drama in one place. However, your website should also be understandable for readers with no knowledge of your audio drama. You should link your website in the show notes of your episodes and in your social media bios. Treat it like the hub for your audio drama.

Your website should include:

- Listening links
- Social media links
- Transcript links
- The cast and crew for each episode
- A press kit (more on this later)
- Information about the show's content
    - short tagline
    - paragraph description
- (Optional) reviews of the show or awards you've won
- (Optional) information about the team behind it

Ideally, the url for your website is your show name or something similar to it, such as "redracula.live" or "sidequestingpod.com." The website layout should also be easy to read, and the information easy to find. Most website creation advice also applies here. I recommend tying your website design into your branding. Use colors that match your cover art and keep the font consistent with your other show graphics. However, never sacrifice legibility for color cohesion. If you need to expand your color pallet to make your website readable, you should do that.

If they're available, you should claim social media handles as soon as you've decided on your show name. As with your website url, your social media handles should be your show name or something like it (such as "redracula" or "sidequestingpod"). Try to claim the same handle across social media sites so it's easy for fans to find you.

Press Kit

Your audio drama should also have a press kit. A press kit is a document (and/or page on your website) that contains all the important info about your show. Having one makes it easy for people unfamiliar with your podcast to learn about it without having to do a lot of searching.

You'd be surprised at how hard it can be, when researching a podcast, to answer questions such as: what genre the show is, is it scripted, who does the sound design, how long are episodes, what is the target audience, what episode to start at, where transcripts can be found . . . I've had to scour a show's website, show notes, and social media before to collect all the information I needed to write about that podcast.

As the curator of a newsletter, I've spent a lot of time looking at podcast press kits while deciding if I want to feature the show. As a casting director, I've spent a lot of time looking at press kits for cast information. As a showrunner, I've spent a lot of time looking at press kits to see who is behind a show and where I can follow them. Usually, I don't know much about a podcast when I'm pulling up their press kit.

You should assume the reader of your press kit is coming in with no prior knowledge of the show. Maybe they're a newsletter curator deciding if they should recommend your show. Perhaps they're a critic wondering if your show should go on a list. Maybe they're a potential listener! Don't be scared to include seemingly obvious facts about your show. The easier it is for people to find info about your podcast, the more likely they are to share and recommend it. You should have one, no matter how small your show is! Don't make people email you for it. Having a link that says "press" or "press kit" on the menu of your website is ideal.

Here's what you should consider including in a press kit:

- Show name and tagline
- A short, one- or two-sentence description
- A longer paragraph-length description
- Episode count and episode length (do you have seasons, or is the podcast "always on"?)
- Where should a first-time listener start?
- Genre and target audience
- Important content warnings for the series as a whole
- Genre and format

- Scripted or unscripted
    - Genre (sci fi, horror, etc.)
    - Make sure to explicitly say that the show is fiction!
- Links to social media accounts
- Link to website
- Contact email
- Downloadable cover art
- Promotional images
    - Social media images
    - Large-format horizontal orientation header images
    - Cast and crew headshots
    - Character art, location art, etc.
- Links to the podcast on podcatchers like Apple, Spotify, PocketCasts, etc.
- Whether the show is independent, produced in partnership with a company, or funded by a company
- Your cast and crew list (with links to their own websites where available)
    - Don't forget to list yourself and your roles too!
- The podcast launch date
- Significant audience data
- Previous press coverage
    - Links to articles and reviews

    - Screenshots or quotes from reviews on Apple, Podchaser, etc.
    - Any awards received
- Where to find transcripts for each episode

If there is anything significant about your show, mention it! Does it focus on a specific type of representation? Perhaps it was made in 24 hours? If something sets you apart from other podcasts, put it in your press kit. Organize the info in whatever way makes the most sense to you. Don't be afraid to explore other shows' press kits for inspiration.

Your title, cover art, website, and press kit are a key part of the marketing and promotion of your audio drama. But they're also important on their own! Even if you're not interested in making time to create a marketing strategy, you should put time into these four things.

Here are some example press kits. You'll see that none of them include everything on the above list.

***Falling Forward* Press Kit:**

Release Date:
Season One: March 1, 2022
Season Two: July 27, 2022

Length: Each season is 10 episodes, 1-4 minutes each

Genre: Science Fiction

Transcripts: Linked on our website.

RSS: pinecast.com/feed/falling-forward

Website: fallingforward.ju.mp

Short Description *Falling Forward* is a sci-fi micro about love, hubris, and coding too close to the sun.

Long Description: *Falling Forward* follows Icarus' efforts to take down Labyrinth Corporation after it's founder, Theseus, stole tech from Icarus' family. Fueled by rage at the death of his aunt Ariadne and ignoring the cautionary advice from his dad Daedalus, Icarus is set on destruction. But will it be the destruction of Labyrinth, or the destruction of Icarus?

Cast and Crew: [lists cast and crew]

Cover Art: [cover art]

***Joy to the World* Press Kit:**

Quick Facts:

Rating: G

Genre: Slice of Life

Episode Length: 3 to 15 minutes

Official Launch Date: Dec 13

Episodes release daily through Dec 24.

Limited series, 12-episode production.

Transcripts released alongside audio.

More Facts:

Tagline: An orbiting holiday audio drama.

About the show: *Joy to the World* follows Joy, an astronaut alone on the ISS, as they take calls from around the world on a lonely Christmas Eve. It's about end-of-year holiday spirit in general, exploring different experiences of what makes this time of year special.

Full Show Credits: [cast and crew for all episodes are listed]

Cover Art: [cover art]

Awards: Award Winner, New Jersey Web Fest 2023. Official Selection, Baltimore Next Media Web Fest 2023. Award Nominee, LA Web Fest 2024.

Re: Dracula Press Kit:

Tagline: A bite-sized audio adaptation of the horror classic.

Launch Date: May 3, 2023.

End Date: November 8, 2023.

Episode Length: Varied.

Downloads & Stats: 2 million and counting. Episodes average 5k listens in the first week. Debuted #2 on the fiction podcast charts! Official selection of 19 film and web festivals.

Description: *Re: Dracula* takes the famous horror tale, breaks it up chronologically (every entry of this epistolary novel has a date), and sends the story directly to your podcatcher as it happens. Every time something happens to the characters, *Re: Dracula* will publish an episode, in as close to real time as it happens. Some episodes will be short (less than a minute), and others will be lengthy (over half an hour). We intend to be a faithful, text-accurate adaptation, featuring a full cast to tug on your heartstrings and sound design to keep you on the edge of your seat.

Press Coverage:
Tor.com's Five Beguiling Gateways Into Gothic Horror
Mentally? A Magpie's Release Day Review
The Gothic Library's *Re: Dracula* Podcast Review
C-schroed's Podcasts I Adore
The Podcast Geek's *Re: Dracula* Review
A Sky Full of Pods' My Experience of *Re: Dracula*

On Racism and Ableism in Dracula: Primarily, we'll be looking at the novel through a modern day lens - not necessarily changing the text, but approaching outdated sections with nuance. We want to experiment with grounded readings of Dracula, the sort of intimate acting that audio drama so often excels at. The majority of the novel will be read as is, including passages that are a product of their time if they are important to the story. However, some derogatory language will be changed, including slurs. Content warnings will always be present.

Inspiration: This project was directly inspired by Dracula Daily - a newsletter that delivers the story into your email inbox. We're big fans of this ingenious way of reading the novel, and we wanted to take it to its natural next step and do a podcast.

Crew: [lists crew]

Cast: [lists cast]

RSS Feed

The RSS feed is what makes a podcast a podcast. The most common way people set up their podcast RSS feed is via a hosting platform, such as Pinecast, Podbean, Buzzsprout, Megaphone, or Acast. There are a lot of options, and they all cost different amounts of money and have slightly different capabilities.

If you're just starting out, you probably don't need anything fancy. Most platforms will give you no trouble uploading an episode that's under an hour, or posting an episode a week (or even daily). If you're planning on making multiple shows that utilize multiple podcasts feeds, it could be useful to find a host that will let you create multiple RSS feeds without additional payment. If you're planning on using dynamic ads (more on that later), you should find a host that is compatible with them.

In general, you should research your options for a podcast host and determine which is the best fit for your needs and your budget. A podcast host that's perfect for one person will be a bad fit for another. It truly boils down to what you want.

To upload your episode, you'll need:

- The episode file as a mp3 file
- A release date and time
- An episode title
- An episode description, also called show notes
- Optionally, episode-specific cover art

Every podcast host I've used has made it easy to upload episodes, and they all have guides for the less technically inclined. Don't stress too much about it; this is probably the easiest part of making an audio drama.

Show Notes

Show notes, or episode description, are the text posted alongside the audio of an episode. This text generally includes a brief summary of the podcast episode, any content warnings, and a link to the transcript of the episode. You can also include guest bios and crew information, links to the podcast website, social media handles, and more.

The art of crafting good show notes is underrated in fiction podcasting. Potential listeners may skim your show notes before deciding to jump into an episode. Subscribers may reference the show notes for all sorts of things.

Your show notes should include:

- Episode description
- Content warnings
- Transcript link
- Cast and crew for that episode
- Links to your show's social media and website
- Any calls to action from the episode itself
- Sentence about how to support the show (with links)

There's no one correct way to format show notes. However, they should generally be simple and clear. Fancy formatting may not correctly reflect across podcast apps. Even bullet points and hyperlinks may not show up. I recommend checking your first episode's show notes across the most popular podcast apps to ensure they are displaying as planned.

Here are some examples of show notes:

What Will Be Here? Episode 1, Go For Deploy.

Jules introduces the team. Suri has doubts about the project. Armani makes their own golden record. Kei is in the ducts. Dane explains how the world is doomed.

Content Notes: contains swearing, the brief presence of fire, recordings of several animal noises, audio of a jet, and the recording of a gunshot. No guns are present in the episode.

TRANSCRIPT: bit.ly/wwbhe1transcript

CREDITS:
Jona Lune (they/them) . . . Jules.
Sahar Iman (they/them) . . . Suri.
Kathy Youssef (they/them) . . . Armani.
Vico Ortiz (they/them) . . . Kei.
John Y. Kamara (he/him) . . . Dane.

This episode was directed and sound designed by Tal Minear (they/them).

Written by Brad Colbroock (they/them/he), Chandler Harrison (she/her), Cole Burkhardt (he/him), Di Reese (she/they), and Tal Minear (they/them).

Intro and outro music by Benny James (she/they).

Transcript by Caroline Mincks (they/them).

ADDITIONAL NOTES: Show Website located at whatwillbehere.crd.co. Social Media is WhatWillBeHere on Twitter and Instagram.

May 3: Jonathan Harker begins his journey.

This episode contains offensive ethnic stereotypes. Transcript here.

This episode featured: Ben Galpin as Jonathan Harker; Ioana Adăscăliței as the Romanian Woman; and Karim Kronfli as Dracula. Directed by Hannah Wright. Dialogue editing by Stephen Indrisano. Sound design by Tal Minear. Featuring music by Travis Reaves. Produced by Ella Watts and Pacific S. Obadiah, with executive producers Stephen Indrisano, Tal Minear, and Hannah Wright. A Bloody FM Production.

Find us online:
Patreon: www.Patreon.com/redracula
Website: www.ReDracula.live
Tumblr: www.tumblr.com/re-dracula
Twitter: twitter.com/bloodyfm
Instagram: Instagram.com/bloody_fm

Someone Dies In This Elevator . . . Depths of Ocotillo Mine
Rating: PG-13.

Enter the depths of the mine, and find out what awaits you. This episode contains generational trauma, discussion of the loss of loved ones, and death in an elevator. Transcript here.

This episode was written by Andrew Siañez-De La O and directed by Newton Schottelkotte. Script editing by Jesse Schuschu. Dialogue editing by Nikko Goldstein and sound design by Tal Minear. Scoring by Tal Minear. Executive produced by Tal Minear. Episode artwork by Tal Minear.

Starring: Jupiter Aispuro as Rosa. Chris Magilton as Mike. Additional voices by Van Winkle, Virginia Spotts, Brad Colbroock, and Tal Minear.

Follow us @SDITEpod on Instagram, Tumblr, and Twitter!

Transcripts

If you make scripted fiction podcasts, you've got a script, which means it's almost no work at all to create and post transcripts. This section will break down why you should have transcripts, how to make them, and where to post them.

Why have transcripts? The biggest reason is that they're an accessibility tool. People who are deaf and hard of hearing, or have auditory processing disorders, or any condition that might make it difficult to engage in an audio-only medium will find transcripts extraordinarily helpful. Some people might use them to listen along with the show. Others might just read them. When you have transcripts, you're expanding the reach of the show and growing your audience.

Transcripts are also helpful for press and podcasts journalists. It's much easier to quickly pull a quote from an episode using a transcript instead of spending an hour listening to it. Fan artists also benefit from having written descriptions of characters or moments. People who are learning the language your show is in will love it. It also benefits your SEO and makes your show easier to find in general.

What makes a script different from a transcript? A script is what's initially written and recorded from. It might have notes for the actors or sound designer, and it might change during production if actors improvise, if scenes are cut, or if a sound designer uses different sound effects. A transcript is essentially a written version of the audio in its final form. If anything deviated from the script during production, it's captured on the transcript.

Usually, making the transcript is the hardest part, but when you've got a script to start with, you're 90% of the way there. Unless you have a script that changed a lot during production, it shouldn't take you more than an hour per 30 minute episode to make the transcript.

Here's what I do:

1. Copy my script into a new document.
2. Play the episode audio.
3. Follow along on the script, updating it to match the audio where needed.
4. Save the document as the episode transcript.

And that's it! If an actor paraphrased a line, I'll change it to match. If my SFX descriptions were a bit vague, I'll add more info. Half the time this process is me changing "SFX: Footsteps" to "SFX: X pairs of footsteps on SURFACE" because I never specify them when I write. I've found I don't need to pause the audio a lot while I follow along, because there's usually not much I need to change. Obviously, mileage will vary per show.

I've learned that it's easier for people to have transcripts as html text or Google documents (as opposed to PDFs), so I usually save my transcripts as Google docs or upload the text directly to the website. Again, PDFs can be difficult for accessibility tools like screen readers to decipher. But if you work with a system that makes this hard, a PDF is okay! Some script formatting makes copy-pasting to a Google doc difficult, and a PDF transcript is truly leagues better than no transcript at all.

You should spend the time to make your script into a transcript. But if this is too big a hurdle for you, just upload the script itself. After all, it's 90% of the way there anyway, and that's something. As long as you're clear about what it is, it's okay.

There are two places you should definitely link your transcripts from: the episode show notes, and your website. This doesn't mean you need to host them there (some podcast apps will cut show notes off after so many characters anyway), just that people should be able to find them from those places. Here are two places you can upload your transcripts to that I hope aren't obsolete by the time you read this.

Google Docs/Google Drive is a great place to put transcripts. You can make a free account for your show, upload transcripts, and share read-only links. If you have PDF transcripts you can use Google Drive, or you can copy them into a Google Doc. A benefit of using a Google Doc is that people who want a PDF can download one, and everyone else can read directly in the Docs or Drive app.

Tumblr is a free option and gives you a more blog-like feel. Their search and tagging functions leave much to be desired, so if you're going this route, I recommend having an external page (such as your website) that links to the transcript for each episode. Otherwise, you'll have to scroll and scroll chronologically.

Chapter 10

Marketing and Promotion

If one of your goals is to have people listening to your audio drama, you're going to have to promote it. This is an entire second job. One of the reasons I strongly recommend producing your entire show before releasing it is that once you're releasing episodes, you can focus on promotion instead of production.

If you're hoping to turn audio drama into a day job, it's worth it to build your brand and start networking early on. Create a website for your audio drama work. Start a newsletter. Collaborate on projects that aren't your own. Take a chance and send that cold email. Be confident in what you know how to do, and humble in learning what you don't.

If you're keeping audio drama as a hobby, you can still do all these things anyway, and I bet you'll get some cool opportunities out of it.

Your Podcast Brand Identity

It's important to build a brand identity for your podcast if you're planning on marketing it. Your brand identity will determine how you market your show. What feelings do you want your audio drama to elicit? How do you want people to think about your show?

The first step in crafting a brand identity is deciding on your target audience. Before you do that, come here and listen closely. Take these next words to heart: Your target audience is not "everyone." Don't try to appeal to the broadest possible audience, because you will fail. I promise, you will fail! Think about who you want most to connect with your work. Who are you creating this audio drama for? That's your target audience. When you promote your podcast, you should be working to market it to them.

To get started defining your target audience, you can create the profile of your ideal listener. This audience persona is a fictional character that embodies your target audience. Build an imaginary biography of someone that loves your show. How old are they? What's their gender? Where do they live, and what do they do for work? How do they relax on the weekends? What's their favorite social media platform? What are their fears? Ambitions? Attitude? What gives them hope? What are they nostalgic for? What are they doing when they listen to podcasts?

This list of questions could go on and on. Once you have this sketched out, give them a name. Now you know who you're making the audio drama for. In general, the more detailed the persona, the clearer the picture of who your target audience is. With a clearer picture of your audience, you will have an easier time engaging them.

Look at different aspects of your audio drama from this ideal listener's perspective. Would they like your cover art? Would this caption on a Tumblr post make them laugh? What calls to action at the end of an episode would engage them?

The audience persona of my ideal listener is a nonbinary person who just graduated from college in California.

They've got a really cool name they gave themself, like Peregrine. They feel a little nostalgic for the simpler times of childhood, which certainly had its problems but also far less responsibility. Peregrine's favorite video game is Skyrim. They like *D&D* but want to try indie rpgs, and their to-read pile is miles long. Peregrine has been on Tumblr since high school and hates Facebook. Their favorite color is purple, but they dye their hair blue then let it fade to green. Peregrine loves the smell of rain but hates overcast days. They drink way too much coffee, and they're worried they'll never find a career they truly love. Peregrine listens to podcasts on their commute and while crocheting on the weekends.

If you feel that your audience isn't properly captured in a single persona, you can make multiple, but I wouldn't recommend more than three. Past that, you'd be best just defining your audience in general with an audience profile.

In an audience profile, you write out characteristics of your target audience in a more generalized fashion. *Sidequesting* is made for young adults, but is intentionally kid-friendly. My target audience is progressive, queer, and nerdy. They probably play video games, like fantasy novels and movies, and are maybe a little bored with day-to-day life. I can tell from my stats that most of the listeners are based in the United States; while I don't make the show for my fellow Americans specifically, this info doesn't surprise me.

Once you've defined your audience, you should also create a tagline for your audio drama. This is a one-sentence description that should get people in your target audience hooked. It's not necessary to name the genre, but it can be helpful. You should avoid descriptors that are too broad.

Simply stating "a fantasy podcast" or "a queer audio drama" isn't enough. Lean on what makes your audio drama different.

Here are some examples:

- *Sidequesting*: "A fantasy podcast about avoiding the main plot"
- *Re: Dracula*: "A bite-sized audio adaptation of the horror classic"
- *Falling Forward*: "A sci-fi micro about love, hubris, and coding too close to the sun"
- *Joy to the World*: "An orbiting holiday audio drama"

This tagline should be the short description of your podcast on RSS feeds and in your social media bios. After the title of your show, this is the second collection of words people will associate your production with. You can scan movie posters to get an idea of good taglines. Which ones draw you in, and which ones tell you nothing?

Once you have a title and tagline, expand it into a longer description. This should be a couple of sentences that explain the premise of the show. A longer description isn't about drawing someone in, it's about convincing someone who has already been drawn in to listen. Think of the back of a book on the shelf.

Here's a few longer descriptions:

- *Sidequesting* is an award-winning scripted fiction podcast about avoiding the main plot and doing sidequests instead. It follows Rion, an adventurer who's willing to help anyone out . . . as long as they're not being asked to deal with the scary wizard that everyone keeps talking about.

- *Re: Dracula* takes the famous horror tale, breaks it up chronologically (every entry of this epistolary novel has a date), and sends the story directly to your podcatcher as it happens. Every time something happens to the characters, *Re: Dracula* will publish an episode, in real time. Some entries will be brief, and others will be long and intense.
- *Falling Forward* follows Icarus' efforts to take down Labyrinth Corporation after its founder, Theseus, stole tech from Icarus' family. Fueled by rage at the death of his aunt Ariadne and ignoring the cautionary advice from his dad Daedalus, Icarus is set on destruction. But will it be the destruction of Labyrinth, or the destruction of Icarus?
- *Joy to the World* follows Joy, an astronaut alone on the ISS, as they take calls from around the world on a lonely Christmas Eve. It's about end-of-year holiday spirit in general, exploring different experiences of what makes this time of year special. This show is completed and out in full . . . check it out now!

You should also decide on a font and color scheme associated with your audio drama. Your cover art should tie into these decisions. While it's not necessary to pull your color scheme directly from your cover art (or vice versa), both should match or fit together. Ideally, *all* the images you post should be easily identified with your podcast. There should be some level of cohesion and consistency. Remember that legibility is always more important than aesthetics, though. Avoid low-contrast colors when it comes to fonts, backgrounds, images, and graphics.

You should also determine posting guidelines for your show accounts. How does your podcast interact with its audience? What adjectives do you want people to use to describe the show? Just like with your personal brand identity, the way you interact as your audio drama will determine how people respond.

Is the voice of your audio drama:

- Mischievous?
- Mysterious or cryptic?
- Comedic?
- Sweet and kind?
- Casual?
- Prim and proper?

This doesn't have to match your own voice or brand identity. A Slice of Life show might lean casual, while a sci-fi tech show may go for a cryptic voice. Comedic audio dramas do well bringing that comedy into their social media posts. Mystery audio dramas might tease clues for their listeners. A family friendly show would do well to keep their posting PG, and a wholesome show would do well to keep their social media wholesome too. In short, you want the audience that enjoys your audio drama to also enjoy the posts about your audio drama.

When it comes to creating a Patreon, running a crowdfunding campaign, or joining a network, you'll find benefits in having a cohesive brand identity. It helps in pitching your show to potential listeners and supporters, and it helps to make it seem like you've got it together and know what you're doing.

Here is the brand sheet I created for *What Will Be Here?*:

Tagline: A sci-fi audio drama about living on a doomed earth (and building things anyway).

Longer Description: 5 friends send a rocket to space with a collection of recordings on it, documenting the world's decline, their experiences living on a doomed earth, the stories they want to tell, and their efforts in building a rocket to get this message to the stars. They wonder what their world will have become by the time their message is listened to. What will be left of a planet that has destroyed itself? What will be left of the people who lived there? What will become of their stories? *What will be here?*

Target Audience: *WWBH* is geared towards Gen-Z and Millennials, especially those who are worried about climate change, unhappy about capitalism, and generally disillusioned with the state of the world. With many openly queer and trans characters, *WWBH* is also geared towards members of the LGBTQ+ community.

Branding Notes: Main colors are cool colors . . . green, teal, blue, purple. Black/grey as background colors, occasional accents of white/beige and red. Trying to hit "down to earth sci-fi" as a vibe. Photo assets include rockets, stars, photos of earth, and archive images from NASA.

Show Voice: Casual and down to earth, like the central characters.

Social Media Guide: Posts are honest and casual, but it's okay to be cryptic about upcoming episodes. Interactions with the audience should always be kind. Reblog space images, posts critical of capitalism, environmental posts, and queer content. Avoid leaning too far into bitterness and "doomsday" posting . . . hope is the central message of *WWBH*.

Social Media Strategy

The social media landscape is ever-changing. What works on one platform may not work on another. Once you decide what social media account(s) you're using, you'll have to do your own research to figure out what will work on that site. Don't chase virality. Instead, foster real engagement with your audience. Ultimately, follower counts are a vanity metric. There's not going to be direct correlation between download numbers and retweets.

I recommend using social media to engage with people already listening to your show instead of bringing new listeners to your show. Most people don't go on social media to find new podcasts. Occasionally they may seek out recommendations from friends or followers, but they're not likely to see a post from an audio drama and immediately listen. They're more likely to see a friend engaging with an audio drama's posts and get interested because of that. It's counterintuitive, but using your social media to interact with your audience may grow your audience more through this sort of osmosis.

The best way to decide which social media sites you should use to market your podcast depends on two factors: what sites your audience uses and what sites you personally use.

You need to meet your audience where they are. This means, for example, you're not getting your Gen Z fan base to join a Facebook group in 2025. Part of knowing your audience is knowing where they hang out online, and what sort of engagement they want. Interact genuinely and avoid pandering. You're not a big company, so you don't need to post like one. It's okay to get a little personal, as long as you maintain boundaries with your audience and vice versa.

Potentially good posts:

- A screenshot of your DAW and some teasers about the upcoming episode
- A picture of your pet doing something cute and therefore for sure helping with production
- Reasonable updates ("Hey everyone, some stuff came up and I have to delay this week's episode!")
- Out of context script screenshots
- Pictures from recording sessions
- An announcement of a download milestone and some thoughts on what it means to you

Potentially bad posts:

- Anything that blames someone specific for delays ("ActorName got their lines in late so you have to wait for this episode")

- Oversharing about your life, either as an excuse or for sympathy
- Negativity about other audio dramas ("We're better than OtherShow because of this!")
- Vague posting about other creators
- Just the episode link, and nothing else about it

You're going to have a better idea of the posting style on a website you visit daily than a new one you're on specifically to share your audio drama. An Instagram-style image might work on Tumblr, but the hashtag culture of Instagram will be wildly out of place on Tumblr. Tumblr's low-key posting style might get you laughs in a Facebook group, but downvoted on Reddit. You'll know things like this intuitively for the websites you already browse. Don't try making an account on every single website. Focus on one or two platforms. You'll either burn out trying to make separate engaging posts on a bunch of them, or fall back into boring, nondescript posts that don't actually help promote your podcast.

When on sites that let you repost/reblog/reshare content, use that feature to complement your original posts. A sci-fi show account could share space facts from NASA. A fantasy show account could share cosplay photos. A show about baking might share recipe links. Follow non-audio drama creators and accounts in your niche and amplify posts from them your audience might like.

Even on more wordy websites, audio dramas who create visuals for their show are usually more successful on social media. They get more engagement and more followers. It's easier to catch people's eyes with fun graphics, and you can tell a lot about the aesthetic of a show from them. Many social media platforms also algorithmically prioritize posts with images. These can be mood boards, in-universe visuals, or even episode-specific cover art. Regarding the latter — most podcast hosts allow you to upload separate cover art for your episodes, and most podcast apps display that cover art alongside the episode. You can make your feed more visually interesting with episode cover art, and as a bonus, you can post that art on social media too. But if that feels overwhelming, fear not — you don't have to do it.

The visuals you post don't all have to be fancy graphics. You can share screenshots of your DAW during sound design, pictures from recording sessions, and even lines from scripts as you write. As a creator, I love to see what's happening behind the scenes on other shows. As a fan, I love getting a teaser for what will be in my podcatcher soon. The process of making art is interesting! The types of visuals that will be a hit are naturally going to vary based on your audience and the algorithms of the social media site you post them on. Knowing your target audience is always key.

It's important to remember that audio dramas and fiction podcasts are evergreen. Episodes don't need to be new to be relevant, interesting, or valid. You don't need to only promote your latest episode; you can (and should!) share old episodes too. There's always going to be people who've just found your show, and content that's old to you will be new and exciting to them. Feel free to jump on online trends or memes to share your audio drama, even if the first episode released five years ago.

When you share episodes on social media, give a direct link to listen. You can use a service that generates a link that will give the clicker options for where to listen, or pick a link that plays well across devices. You can also just use your website!

In general, you should reduce the number of clicks people have to do to engage with what you post. Don't make them search your show up in a podcast app, or Google your merch store, or scour your website for a Patreon link. Put something in the post that people can use to get where you want them to go.

However, avoid just dropping a link to an episode or your Patreon and running off. Social media is about engagement, so you need to *engage*. Talk about the creation of the episode, or share some fun facts about what happens. People who haven't listened to your audio drama are likely to come across your posts, so it will be beneficial to add context for them. And people who *have* listened are more likely to share the post if it has context.

Like with your website, you should make it so that newcomers to your show can see what your audio drama is about from the social media profile alone. With all things, you need to make it easy to find and learn about your podcast. Put your tagline in the bio and add a link to your website. If a site allows for pinned posts, pin an informational post about your audio drama.

In all things marketing, you should lower the barrier for people to discover your podcast.

Privacy and Safety

Making an audio drama means you're part of the entertainment industry. You're putting your name out there in a new or different way. RSS feeds are public and publicly show information like which email address you used to set up your feed. Your audio drama will be available almost everywhere. And people can be WEIRD.

I recommend having a separate email for your audio drama activities, be it a show email (podcastname@gmail.com) or a different personal email (yournamepods@gmail.com). If you're able to, I'd also recommend getting a custom domain, so your show email can be yourname@podcastname.com. People will get a hold of your email, be it to request interviews on your podcast (yes, on your scripted fiction podcast), sell their cool new podcast tech, or complain about your content warnings. Despite the spam, you don't want to be unreachable, because legitimately cool opportunities and collaborators will end up in your inbox too.

Keeping podcast emails to one address minimizes the chances of bad actors getting a hold of the email you use for your banking and password manager, but allows the coordination and communication necessary for production. As a bonus, you can step back from the podcast work in your inbox, while still keeping tabs on personal mail whenever you need a break.

Something else you should consider is working under a pen name. This can be your legal first name and a different last name, or something entirely new. I wish I did this, and I'm too far into my audio drama career to change it. This means anyone Googling my name can find my podcasts, and I have little options with regard to keeping spheres of my life separated. I'm forever doomed to having my engineering coworkers ask about my audio dramas. You can avoid this now! Learn from my mistakes! Depending on where you live, there may be some legal forms where you need to clarify the difference between your "doing business as" name and your legal name, especially where money is involved. Be sure to do your own research on those things, especially if you want to ensure contractors aren't privy to your legal name.

All the standards of online safety apply here as well. Assume anything you post on social media is there forever. Assume anyone can use personal information you share for nefarious means . . . and the bigger your audio drama gets, the more likely someone will try. There are downsides to fame, even niche audio drama level fame. Proceed carefully from the get-go so that you worry less when shit hits the fan.

Here's a personal story. In 2022, I was at a podcast conference. So was Ben Shapiro, without a badge. (If you don't know who this is, I am genuinely jealous of you). I tweeted about it, and it went a semi-viral. Shapiro even included screenshots of my tweets, username included, in a segment on his *Daily Wire* show. As a result of this virality, I received a deluge of harassment from his fans that lasted multiple weeks. Some things that happened:

- Some right wing influencers entering the conference without a badge, camera in tow
- Being added to 20+ lists on Twitter either insulting me or threatening me
- Before I had locked my account, terrible comments on my recent tweets

- Two weeks of constant username tagging on vitriolic tweets by right wing users
- Negative reviews of the audio dramas I had tagged in my twitter bio
- Emails to the account I had listed on my website full of nasty things
- More emails "submitting" to my newsletter also full of nasty things
- Harassment on Instagram, because my username was similar there
- Tweets to podcast organizations they thought I worked with calling for me to be fired
- Reposting of edited version of pictures I had shared, including my profile picture

Here's some things I did right:

- Already had two factor authentication on all my accounts
- Did not list my current job on LinkedIn, which meant trolls could not contact my employer
- Did not have a picture of myself on my Twitter profile (instead an avatar I had commissioned)
- Only had my first name displayed next to my username (Tal @starplanes)
- Locked my Twitter quickly, and later temporarily changed the username
- Deleted my Twitter bio, which had my city, podcasts, and a website link in it

- My Instagram was already private, but I soon permanently changed the username
- Had not previously shared where I was staying during the conference and the events I was planning to attend — friends escorted me to my last presentation on stage
- Ensured my friends would not accidentally publicize my whereabouts during the conference or the details of my flight home
- Ran blocklists on Ben Shapiro and Matt Walsh's followers (auto blocking many of the people tweeting at me)

Here's some things I wish I had done:

- Not had my city in my Twitter bio, even though it was a big city
- Had a different username on my Instagram, a personal account I rarely posted podcasting stuff on
- Held conference organizers accountable during the event, as they unfollowed and ignored me afterwards

I share this breakdown as a sort of "worst case scenario" for what can happen online, especially when the in-person and online worlds combine. Have precautions in place for when things get weird. Don't assume it won't happen to you.

Your Own Brand Identity and Parasocial Relationships

When you're selling the idea of your show, you're also selling the idea of yourself. Intentional or not, the way you interact with fans and creators will build a brand, somewhat tied to the brand of your show but not exclusively so.

You should think about how you want people to perceive you and your work. What adjectives do you want people to describe you with?

Are you:

- businesslike and professional
- friendly and approachable
- hip and cool
- aloof and mysterious
- weird and artsy
- direct and no-nonsense
- silly and fun
- harsh and intimidating

Ultimately, it matters less what you actually are, but what people perceive you as. When you grow your show, people are going to get an idea of you in their heads that is not you. They might get attached to that idea, project onto it, and leave you feeling . . . well, kind of weird about the whole thing.

Parasocial relationships are one-sided relationships where one person extends emotional energy, interest, and time, and the other person is unaware of the first's existence (or only aware of them in a very limited capacity, such as "that person with the cat avatar who comments on my social media posts"). Parasociality is not inherently a bad thing, but can become so when boundaries are crossed. Think of someone stalking a celebrity, or a celebrity messaging a fan inappropriately. Both situations arise from parasocial relationships.

In indie audio drama, most shows start small, and therefore the creators start out very approachable. Fans have no trouble interacting with the maker of their new favorite audio drama, sharing fan art and getting their questions answered. Because a fan can readily get a response from a creator, it's easier for them to imagine that the creator is their friend, and easier for them to get invested in their idea of that creator.

They may feel they know the creator of the audio drama they love, when in reality they only know *a small part of* that creator. This fan may form expectations of the creator based on a warped idea of them, and react emotionally when those expectations are not reached. The creator, having no idea of these expectations and not knowing the ideals their fan has projected on them, will find this very unexpected and alarming.

This isn't the only way parasocial relationships between fans and creators can play out in audio drama, but it's one example.

In general, it's easier to be personal with 20 fans than with 200, and easier to be personal with 200 fans than with 2,000 (and so on). The more personal and open you are with your fans, the easier it is for them to develop a parasocial relationship with you. It's easy to think that nobody would form a weird attachment to you or obsession with your work, but it can happen to anyone. But as I said before, parasocial relationships are not inherently bad as long as boundaries are respected and nothing feels *off*. Just be aware that you

may acquire fans that have an idea of you that isn't quite you, and handle any peculiar reactions of theirs with grace.

As an audio drama creator, it's also important to act professionally with other creators, collaborators, and fans. The lines are easily blurred, especially for friends collaborating on a podcast. Just as with fans, you should be wary of crossing boundaries and approach interactions with creators respectfully. Within the audio drama scene, it's easy for fans to become creators, and creators to become collaborators. You might find yourself collaborating with a producer whose work you admire. Maybe you'll be that person with admirable work someone else is excited to collaborate with. Parasocial relationships have the potential to turn into real social relationships.

Fan Spaces

If you're managing a fan space (like a Discord server), it's also important to lay out a code of conduct for that space. This code of conduct should create ground rules for interaction and outline the response for when those rules are broken. Without moderation, large fan spaces are likely to spiral out of control. If this happens in a space you moderate, this will reflect badly on you. If a space you manage is getting too large to deal with, it's okay to close the "official" space and let fans create their own.

Here are rules I made for a small, low-key space:

1) Be nice. Respect people, use their correct pronouns, and don't be a jerk. 2) No hate speech, bullying, or sexual harassment. 3) Swearing is a-okay, but please keep this server generally safe for work. 4) If an episode has just aired, keep discussion of it in the spoiler channel for a week to give people a chance to catch up.

If you engage in hate speech, bullying, or harassment you will be removed from the server immediately, possibly without a warning. If you feel you've been unreasonably removed you can DM me. If I've blocked you, it means you really messed up and you should think about what you did. If you're generally not being nice/respectful I will message you with a warning, but if your behavior continues you will be removed from the server. If you post NSFW, I'll ask you to stop. If you keep posting NSFW, you'll be removed from the server. If you accidentally spoil things, I'll remove your post and direct you to the proper channel. If you intentionally go around spoiling things, you'll be removed from the server.

Here are a different set of rules I utilized for a bigger space:

Be nice or I'll remove you. No spamming or hate speech, and stay on topicish. Do not post the same link in different channels, that counts as spam. If you wish to share a lot of information or links in a short amount of time, do so in a thread.
Spoiler guard all spoilers outside of the spoiler-zone channel. If it's not been in this year's Dracula Daily Email, it's a spoiler.

No NSFW stuff as there may be minors here. (This includes NSFW jokes). Swearing is acceptable as long as it is not directed at a person. Please avoid innuendos.

Some of the cast and most of the Re: Dracula crew is in this server. Don't post things you don't want them to see. You are most welcome to make fan-only spaces outside of this server.

Mods may step in if the conversation is getting close to breaking the rules . . . consider this a redirection of the conversation and not a reprimand.

- *If you break the rules by accident, you'll be given a gentle warning. Mistakes happen!*
- *Consistent breaking of rules (ex: often being unkind, posting multiple NSFW innuendos, etc) will get you a formal warning, and if you continue you will be removed from the server.*
- *Some actions, such as spamming (especially sharing scammy links) or harassing users will get you removed without a warning.*

Networks

Podcast networks can be many things, and joining one can help or hurt your growth. A network might be a group of independent shows that promote each other's work. It might be a company that organizes and sells dynamic ads for all shows on the network. It could be a production group that actively produces the shows on the network. Or anything in between!

Because of this variety, it is important to understand what a podcast network will do for you before agreeing to join it. If a network does not provide a contract, run. I'm serious! It doesn't have to be a complicated contract full of legalese. But the expectations for what you need to do and what the network needs to do should be clearly laid out. You should know how disputes will be handled and what to do when things go wrong.

Multiple times, I have seen a podcast "network" attempt to claim that a show and IP belong to them when a creator tried to leave. It is absolutely imperative that you have the structure for leaving a network laid out in writing before you formally join. Otherwise, things will get very messy. They can get messy even with a contract! A particularly litigious podcast network has threatened to sue several creators when they tried to leave the network, going so far as to utilize NDAs to prevent negative discussion of the company.

I say this not to fearmonger, but to illustrate that you need to proceed with caution when sharing your work and brand identity with a second party. There are certainly some great benefits to joining a network. I've gotten monthly ad revenue by joining a network and inserting dynamic ads. My shows have grown utilizing cross promotion within my network. I've had some marketing help on social media as well.

Many networks will require a certain number of monthly downloads before allowing a show to join. Some may require shows on the network to be a certain genre (for example, horror). Others have neither requirement. The best way to find out what you need for a specific network is to ask — many will have a contact email and even say how to apply on their website. The best way to find out which networks exist is by listening to shows and speaking with creators. It's not likely that a network will approach you (unless your show is very big), so you should be reaching out to networks if joining one is a goal.

Festivals and Awards

Film and web festivals are expanding into fiction podcasting. It seems like every other year a new awards crop up proclaiming themselves "the Oscars of podcasting." Is entering worth it? Well, it depends on your goals.

Film and web fests usually have lower entry fees compared to formal podcasting awards. This is in part because they are targeting indie creatives (whereas other awards are targeting production companies). There's rarely a popular vote component to these awards, which means your work is being judged simply on its merit and not its fanbase. Each festival has different judges, which means different responses. I had a work win "Best Fantasy Audio Drama" at one web festival and not be selected for consideration in another.

I find that film and web fests are almost always worth it if you can attend the event itself. There are a lot of networking opportunities, and it's also just a fun experience. If you can't attend, it can be hit or miss. Some festivals have subcategories by genre ("Best Fantasy Show") or role ("Best Sound Design"), but others only have "Best Podcast." The more subcategories there are, the higher your chances of winning an award. Also, the more well known the festival is, the more eyes you will get on your project, though in general festival wins won't impact your download numbers. However, it is a treat to refer to your work as an award-winning audio drama.

For other awards, it's worth comparing the entry fee to what you gain from winning. Some awards may have a grant for their winners. Others may not even have a trophy. When deciding whether to submit for an award, look up previous winners and see where they're at now. Find out if you think these shows are actually good. Did the awards company promote their finalists? Are the awards themselves well run? Or does it seem like a scam? You can easily spend thousands of dollars on entry fees and get nothing for it.

Check in with yourself on what your goals are. Do you want validation from panels of judges? Do you want one award for your website? Are you out for a specific award? Don't feel like you need to submit because it's the thing to do. There's no guarantee this will grow your audience, help get you a book/tv deal, or land you on a better network. Simply put, you might just get an award. If that's not your goal, you might not even need to bother with awards.

The awards landscape is constantly changing. New awards are cropping up just as fast as others are dying out. If you're considering running the festival circuit or submitting to other awards, it's worth checking in with other creators to see what's working for them. You might discover a gem of a webfest!

Where to Advertise

You might have the funds to dedicate a budget to marketing. But what's the best way to spend it? The answer varies based on how much money you have and who your target audience is.

Usually, social media ads don't go very far. They're easy to ignore, annoying users more often than interesting them. You're likely to get a better return on your investment by just posting on social media and relying on organic growth. Ads within podcast apps work a little better, because you're automatically reaching podcast listeners, likely on the app they would use to subscribe to your show.

Podcasting newsletters are a popular choice for advertisements. These newsletters go out to people who want to keep up with new podcasts and may be actively looking for new shows. Some newsletters are happy to share new shows or new seasons for free. You can also pay for ads on other podcasts . . . or arrange for a promo swap.

Feed Drops and Promo Swaps

A podcast feed drop is when you drop an episode of another show onto your own RSS feed. Usually this is followed by that podcast dropping an episode of your show on their feed. When this happens, audiences from your show discover the show you've shared on your feed, and vice versa. Done right, this tactic will bring new listeners to your audio drama.

You can do feed drops whenever you want to. I tend to do one feed drop per month or fewer, but in the course of releasing your show, you might find that something different works better.

Some creators will use feed drops as a "replacement" for a normal episode. For example, if you're traveling/sick/busy and can't meet your normal upload schedule, you can stick a feed drop in on your standard release date to give your audience something to listen to. Upload schedules tend to be fairly fluid in audio drama, so something like this is not expected by listeners. Personally, I'll do feed drops more or less when my heart desires it.

The length a feed drop is kept up varies, and should be something you discuss with the person whose podcast you're sharing. I usually keep mine up for about a month, because I do monthly feed drops and I like having one on the feed at a time. Some people might want to keep another show's episode up for a shorter or longer time. For example, sometimes you'll have a smaller show swapping with a bigger show, and the smaller show will leave the drop on longer to acquire more downloads. As long as you communicate your plan, you can basically do what you want.

It took me a while to think of an RSS feed as a malleable thing. You're allowed to delete things. You can rearrange the order of bonus episodes. It doesn't have to stay static, as you initially uploaded it, forever. So don't be scared to take a feed drop down after it's had its time to shine. It can also be helpful, at the end of your scheduled feed drop, to let the show know how many downloads they got on your feed.

When deciding which shows to do feed drops with, you should pick ones that have something in common with your show! For my lighthearted fantasy audio drama, I like to swap with shows that are lighthearted, fantasy, kid-friendly, or have actor overlap. But even within audio drama, audiences listen to all sorts of genres, so I wouldn't discount "fiction" as being a thing in common!

I also keep all this in mind for trailer swaps, also called promo swaps. Instead of placing an entire episode of another show on your feed, you share a trailer for another podcast at the beginning or end of your episode. In exchange, that podcast will put a trailer for your show at the beginning or end of one of their episodes. It has all the same benefits of a feed drop, allowing audiences to discover new shows (and allowing to you grow your own listener base). It's just a slightly different way to go about exchanging promos between shows.

Approaching a show for a feed drop or promo swap is as simple as asking them nicely. It's okay to cold-email shows as long as you do it kindly. You might get a no — maybe their show isn't in a place for feed drops, maybe the creator is too busy to coordinate one, maybe they don't think you're a good fit. But it doesn't hurt to ask! Rejection is just part of the game.

General Tips

The longer a show goes on, the bigger the audience will be. By keeping up with production, chances are your audio drama audience will grow. The most potent marketing tactic in podcasting is word of mouth. When people like a show, they tell their friends. If you don't have the time or resources to dedicate to marketing, don't stress. Focus on making a good audio drama, and it may grow slowly, but it will grow.

We're still in the early stages of audio drama. The landscape has always been dramatically changing and probably will continue to do so. Don't be afraid to try new things, re-try old things, and abandon ideas that simply aren't working.

Nothing is set in stone when it comes to marketing your audio drama.

Keep in mind that the shiny new social media site everyone is hopping on might be old news in a matter of months, or that your reliable old social media site might be bought by a billionaire and run into the ground. The effort you put into growing an audience on social media is always owned by someone else.

If you have the capacity to manage a newsletter, you should do it! Running a newsletter lets you put show updates directly into your audience's email inbox. You're not beholden to algorithms or word counts, and it can be one of the best ways to engage with fans of your work.

Chapter 11

Funding and Revenue

Making money from your audio drama is one of the harder goals to have, but that doesn't mean you shouldn't try. There are several options for fundraising, and you can pursue multiple of them.

Ways to Fund an Audio Drama:

- Crowdfunding campaign
- Patreon/Ko-Fi/other monthly subscription
- Grants or other sponsorship
- Dynamic ads
- Host-read ads
- Merch

Crowdfunding campaigns, Patreon subscriptions, and dynamic ads are the most popular ways of getting revenue for an audio drama. Some audio dramas will utilize all three. Many shows have merchandise available, but usually it doesn't bring in significant income unless there is a *very* large and engaged fanbase. Grants and other sponsorships are hit or miss, and will likely vary depending on your location.

Crowdfunding Campaigns

Crowdfunding campaigns are a one-time sprint to fund an audio drama. They run anywhere between two weeks and two months, and are frequently done utilizing a platform like Kickstarter or Indiegogo. A goal is set, supporters get rewards for chipping in, and the platform usually takes about 5%. There's no single right way to crowdfund, but there are some good rules of thumb to abide by.

Before you even begin to prepare for your own crowdfunding campaign, you should take a look at other podcast crowdfunds — and not just successful ones, but also those that didn't hit their goal. What about these campaigns would have made you interested in supporting them? Is there anything more you wish you knew about the podcasts? Check out what these podcasters did to market their fundraising campaigns and see if anything speaks to you.

It's also essential to know your target audience and appeal directly to them when you crowdfund. Where do they get their news? How do they find new podcasts? Which social media platforms do they favor? What catches their interest? Have answers to these questions! If you don't do your research, you're setting yourself up for failure. Ideally, you have most of these questions already answered from when you worked out your brand identity.

Even before your crowdfunding campaign starts, engaging with your audience and marketing your podcast will set you up for success. More people following your work means more people following your crowdfund. Especially for a new podcast, building hype and a following pre-campaign is important. Remember that it's not enough to simply create a crowdfunding page. You need to draw people to it.

Be sure to familiarize yourself with the available crowdfunding platforms before you set your page up. The fees may vary, and some platforms require a minimum goal (usually $500). It's worth talking to other creators who have crowdfunded to learn what worked for them. Did they like the platform they used? What did they do to engage their audience?

Fixed vs. Flexible Funding Goals

On some platforms, you need to hit your goal to keep any of the funds raised. This is called fixed funding. Some platforms allow you to keep any money you raise, no matter how small. This is called flexible funding. The goal you set should depend on whether you are utilizing a platform with fixed or flexible funding. If you don't need to reach your full goal to keep the funds, you're safe setting a higher one. But if you need to reach your full goal, you should consider setting a lower overall goal and using stretch goals for anything that isn't strictly needed to produce your audio drama.

An important question to think about is: "*Will you be making this show regardless of whether or not you hit your goal?"* If the answer is yes, consider utilizing a platform with flexible funding and setting a goal that matches your budget. This informs the audience of what the audio drama costs to make. Be sure to have a backup plan for what happens if you don't reach your goal. This might be shorter episodes, a smaller season, less sound design, a longer production time frame, or something else.

If you're only going to make the audio drama if you hit your goal, utilize fixed funding. Your goal should be the minimum of what you need to make your show. It can be difficult to take the fixed funding risk, but it may be necessary if you intend on paying fair wages to your cast and crew.

Audio dramas that utilize fixed funding are more likely to hit their goals. This is in part due to the fact that shows with flexible funding can set more ambitious goals without consequence, but also in part due to the psychology of crowdfunding. If a show with a $5k fixed goal is $4k funded, people want to support the show to ensure it gets made. If a show with a $10k flexible goal is $4k funded, people may see that the show will be made regardless and decide their support isn't needed.

When setting your goal, don't forget to factor in the cost of platform fees and physical rewards. It's also important to include yourself in the budget. The goal you set should match the cost of production. If the cost of production is too high, it's often better to scale back on the complexity and length of the podcast than to pay people less — yourself included! Use crowdfunding to make your podcast sustainable.

Timing and Duration

I recommend against holding a campaign in December (as people are focused on holiday spending) or January (as people are recovering from holiday spending). Lots of horror audio dramas crowdfund in October, and many others choose late spring and early summer. What month you pick doesn't correlate directly to the success of your campaign. It can be useful to keep an eye on the frequency of crowdfunding campaigns when you're planning your own. If there are 7 audio drama campaigns currently running, it might be difficult to get eyes on your campaign.

Most campaigns run for about 30 days. Running your crowdfunding campaign for longer doesn't mean you'll get more money. There's typically a spike in support when your campaign starts and when it ends, with a plateau of trickling donations in between. Crowdfunding takes a lot of effort on the part of the showrunner, and it can be difficult to sustain this effort for more than a month.

Some platforms may give you the ability to extend your campaign. If you're getting increased support in the second half of your campaign, extending it might make a difference. Extending a campaign that has gotten no support won't make it suddenly get donations.

When crowdfunding, you should have enough of your audio drama finished in order to share a proof of concept. This could be a trailer or pilot episode. Even if it's not the final audio of the podcast, I recommend having *something* people can listen to. It should match the tone and production level of your audio drama. Crowdfunding is pitching your work to potential supporters. It's crucial to have something for them to get excited about, and to show that you're capable of making the podcast.

The Crowdfunding Page Itself

On the crowdfunding page, you should have basic information about your podcast, including the fact that it *is* a podcast. You can't assume that everyone who comes across your crowdfunding campaign is familiar with your work. What is the show about, and who would like it? Have a tagline near the top to get people hooked.

But a one-sentence description of your show isn't enough on its own. After the tagline, you should have a longer explanation of the show. Consider comparing it to other media: "If you liked this movie and this book, you'll like this audio drama." Remember that while you know all the intricate details of your production, someone looking at your page starts off knowing nothing.

You should also explain how many episodes you'll make if you hit your goal, and where the money is going. Having a budget breakdown on your page is crucial. You're asking people for money, so make sure you're telling them how it's going to be spent.

The brand identity you worked out for the marketing and promotion of your audio drama will be crucial in the marketing and promotion of your crowdfunding campaign. For example, good art will draw people's eyes and help your campaign succeed. Ideally, people should be able to guess that a graphic is for your podcast before reading it. A cohesive crowdfunding page, with matching fonts and images, shows an eye for details that backers assume will extend to the show itself. If your Kickstarter page looks beautiful, the show will sound beautiful too, right?

Having a brand identity is important because the more put together and professional your production seems, the more people will be willing to support it. Potential backers want to feel confident their money is going towards a podcast that will not simply be made, but be made *well*.

If your podcast pitch boils down to "trust me," chances are it's not going far. If a friend-of-a-friend came up to you one day and said, "I've never made a video game before, but I have this really cool idea, I just need some money. It's about gays in space. That's all I've got so far, but it's going to be awesome," would you be excited to give them money? Would you believe funding this nebulous gays in space video game is worth it?

One aspect of many crowdfunding platforms is to create a crowdfunding video. This video should be 2 minutes or less; most people will stop watching after 30 seconds. It's a great opportunity to include your proof of concept audio so that viewers will know what the show sounds like by watching your crowdfund video. I recommend including interesting visuals. Avoid a still image of your cover art. Make sure that the video includes a call to action to support the campaign. You should explain why people should pledge to the crowdfund. What are they getting out of it?

Here's example copy from the crowdfunding page for *Re: Dracula*:

Re: Dracula is a bite-sized audio adaptation of the horror classic *Dracula*.

We're taking the famous horror tale, breaking it up chronologically (every entry of this epistolary novel has a date), and sending the story directly to your podcatcher as it happens. Every time something happens to the characters, *Re: Dracula* will publish an episode, in as close to real time as possible. The first episode will drop May 3, and the final episode, November 7th. Some entries will be brief, and others will be long and intense.

We intend to be a faithful, text-accurate adaptation, featuring a full cast to tug on your heartstrings and sound design to keep you on the edge of your seat. We'll have content warnings at the top of each episode, and while we aim to follow the text of the novel as much as possible, we will be removing unnecessary racist asides. But primarily, we'll be looking at the novel through a modern day lens . . . not changing the text, but approaching outdated sections with nuance. In *Re: Dracula*, we want to experiment with grounded readings of *Dracula*, the sort of intimate acting that audio drama so often excels at.

This project was directly inspired by *Dracula Daily* . . . a newsletter that delivers the story into your email inbox. We're big fans of this ingenious way of reading the novel, and we wanted to take it to its natural next step and do a podcast. The show will be released for free, but those who help us fund the project will get additional perks, including ad-free episodes, a full audiobook, digital downloads, and more!

If you like:

- Getting emails from your good friend Jonathan Harker

- Yelling at Dr. Seward for his medical crimes
- Oddly soothing horror audio drama
- More vampires in your life
- Immersive sound design
- Full cast voice acting
- Independent audio fiction

we think you'll like this show!

Cast: [List of cast members and who they are voicing]

Crew: *Re: Dracula* is produced by Tal Minear, Hannah Wright, Stephen Indrisano, Ella Watts, and Pacific Obadiah. Between us, we've worked on podcasts including *Doctor Who Redacted*, *Inn Between*, *Sidequesting*, *Someone Dies In This Elevator*, *What Will Be Here?*, *The Orphans*, and more! This isn't our first show or our first time crowdfunding. We know exactly what's in store when it comes to producing this show, and we're excited about it!

Perks: For supporting the show, you can get such goodies as:

- The full *Re: Dracula* audiobook
- Access to exclusive Discord channels in the show server
- Bonus audio, including a compilation of Dracula memes read by our voice actors
- A digital calendar that details episode drops

- A shout-out on social media
- A Dracula Recipe Zine
- *Re: Dracula* stickers
- A postcard from Dracula Castle
- A TTRPG digital bundle of vampire-themed games
- An exclusive t-shirt
- A friendship bracelet from Jonathan Harker
- A thank you in the show audio

Budget: Here's our budget breakdown: [pie chart with budget breakdown]

Stretch Goals:

- $15k: Original Music
- $20k: Bonus Episodes
- $25k: Concept Album

Other Ways To Help:

Can't support the show monetarily? You can help us tremendously by spreading the word about our campaign!

- Like/Share/Comment on our social media posts to please the algorithm, and tag people on your social media posts and ask them to share the campaign!
- Share our trailer on your podcast!
- Write a blog post about the show!

- Tell your friends about how much you love the show!
- Tell your enemies about how much you hate the show!

Telling everyone you know about it will absolutely make a difference, especially if you tell them why you think they should support us.

Perks

When creating perks for those who support your crowdfunding campaign, you should utilize as many digital perks as possible. These perks can be something like letting a backer name a character in the show, being thanked on the website or in the credits, or getting annotated scripts. You don't have to match the theme of your podcast, but it's going to be more fun and exciting for supporters if you do.

Digital perks are easier to fulfill and require no shipping costs. In general, you shouldn't spend a lot of money on rewards, especially up front. Most people support an audio drama crowdfunding campaign for the show itself, not the rewards — but having good rewards can sway them to support at a higher tier!

For physical perks, I recommend having photos of the items on your page so that people know what they're signing up to get. Getting product samples (or just ordering low quantities initially) can be a good way to do that. Stickers are a popular physical perk and can be shipped in a standard envelope.

The best advice I have is for you to have perks that you personally are excited about, and if you can tie them into the theme of the show, even better. Name the different tiers something fun that relates to your audio drama.

Here are some ideas for crowdfunding perks:

- Name a character or place in the show
- Thanks on the website or in an episode's credits
- Annotated scripts
- Social media shout out
- Tarot card reading
- Bonus episode
- Bloopers
- Ad-free or early episodes
- Desktop or phone wallpapers
- Invitation to a launch party
- Stickers of show or character art
- Postcards, tarot cards, trading cards
- T-shirt or mug with art or a quote

A lot of podcasters overlook the value of a low-price tier in their crowdfunding campaign. If your first tier is at $20, you're going to miss out on a lot of support. Lots of people are willing to support new podcasts, but don't necessarily have $20 to give. Even if you get just 10 people supporting a $5 tier, that's $50 you didn't have to begin with. It adds up! Be sure to also include a high tier of $500 or $1000. You never know if someone is going to go for it, so ensure the opportunity is there.

You should be aiming for a decent gap between each tier, with something new and exciting being offered for each one. Avoid having too many options, as people tend to get overwhelmed beyond 7 tiers. Having as few as 3 can still work perfectly, as long as you maintain a fair spread of costs and variety of perks.

Promotion

The most crucial and most tiring part of running a crowdfunding campaign is getting the word out. Post about it on social media! Email your friends and family! Tell as many people about it as possible! If people don't know about your podcast, they can't help you fund it. If people know about your podcast but don't know you're crowdfunding, they still can't help you fund it. More eyes on your campaign means more donations to it.

Tell people about your show. Who's making it? Who are the characters in it? What is it about? I recommend posting on social media at least once a day about your campaign, if not more. Every post you make will not show up on every single follower's feed or dashboard. However, avoid overusing tagging or using bots at all. Your posts should be genuine and not spammy.

Here are some promotion tactics you can do:

- Share your crowdfund on your podcast feed

- Post on social media
- Message friends and family
- Call your grandparents
- Email podcast newsletters
- Cross promote with other podcasts
- Reach out to local media
- Put signs up in your city
- Hold a livestream event
- Host a party
- Do a giveaway
- Hold a contest
- Make some memes
- Create milestones and publicly celebrate reaching them

The best way to promote your crowdfund is to contact your friends and family with personalized messages. People you already know are more likely to support you. Don't send a generic message with a bunch of people copied — write out something specific and personal explaining your project, why they might like it, and what it would mean to have their support. This is much more time-consuming than generic social media posts, but it will have a greater return on your investment.

It's also useful to make graphics to share when promoting your campaign. They don't need to be super professional, either — a silly meme can go a long way. I liked having a mix of well-worded posts and less well-worded shitposts coming from my social media accounts. Having fun is great for your stress levels and your social media engagement!

To avoid exhaustion, do as much as you can in advance. Consider making graphics and scheduling social media posts before the campaign goes live. Organize your cross promotion with other podcasts the month before your campaign starts. While your crowdfund is running, be sure to take breaks. You don't need to be promoting it 24/7, and you will burn out if every waking moment is dedicated to your campaign.

Consider leaving a gap in your production schedule for crowdfunding if you're doing both at the same time. It's hard to sound design an episode and coordinate a recording session and manage a crowdfunding campaign. Running a crowdfunding campaign for one season of an audio drama is like cramming a year's worth of Patreon work into two months (more on Patreon soon).

You will have more success with crowdfunding if you have a preexisting audience. Crowdfunds by established creators, or for additional seasons of a show, are more successful because of this. A new audio drama by a first time creator will start with a small audience. As a result, fewer people will support a crowdfunding campaign, let alone even be aware of it.

The Subscription Model

Using a subscription model is like taking the stress of a crowdfunding campaign and diluting it over the entire year. Instead of a one time donation, you're asking fans to give a smaller amount monthly. The most popular platform for this type of model is Patreon, so I'll be using it as a catch-all term for subscription platforms. The second most popular subscription platform for audio drama creators (at least in 2026) is probably Ko-Fi. If you're considering going the subscription route, I encourage you to do your own research on the best platform for your needs.

The perks for joining a Patreon can be similar to supporting a crowdfunding campaign: access to behind the scenes content or bonus audio, mailed stickers or other goodies. But because a subscription is recurring, you should provide recurring benefits. A backlog of content is a great asset for recent Patrons, but you should plan for new content for the supporters who have been with you for a while. It's a balancing act between making content for the Patreon and content for the show itself. There's no easy answer for how to allocate your time and energy.

The key to having a successful Patreon is to act like you have a successful Patreon before you do. It needs to be a priority . . . and seem like it's a priority for supporters. Compare your tiers to other subscriptions out there, like Netflix or Spotify. What makes their subscriptions worth it? How can you do the same for the subscription you are providing?

When making a Patreon (or other subscription) page, consider having a low, medium, and high tier. More than 3 options will likely over-complicate things. Keep in mind that no matter how good your page is, people will cancel their subscriptions. It's not always your fault — situations and budgets can change at the drop of a hat. If possible, I recommend utilizing an exit survey to see why subscriptions are canceled. Many subscription platforms like Patreon have this option built in. This data can let you know where you're going wrong (if you *are* going wrong).

You should be consistently promoting your Patreon. Include a link in every episode's show notes. Shout it out at the end of episodes. Post about it on your social media. The repetition will help you gain subscribers. I included a link to the show Patreon in the show notes of every episode on *Re: Dracula*, and when I ran an audience survey, I found out that 15% of listeners didn't know we had a Patreon. Clearly I needed to do more promotion.

The *Re: Dracula* Patreon has two tiers, one at $5 and one at $10. I've named the first Vampire Moth and the second Vampire Bat, in keeping with the Dracula theme.

Both tiers get:

- Early access to bonus episodes
- Access to a Patreon-exclusive miniseries where I read and discuss a terrible gothic novel
- Behind the scenes posts about production happenings
- Access to a patron only discord server
- Some free digital downloads, like desktop backgrounds and a coloring book

The higher tier gets:

- A monthly Q&A episode where their questions get answered

- A copy of the *Re: Dracula* and *Re: Carmilla* audiobooks
- Free digital downloads of everything in our Patreon shop

I've found the hardest part of running a Patreon is consistently creating new content that makes the subscription worth it.

Common Patreon perks include:

- Ad free episodes
- Early episode access
- Blooper Reels
- Interviews with cast and crew
- Patreon-exclusive episodes
- Behind the scenes posts
- Monthly live streams with showrunners
- A patron-exclusive discord server

In truth, you can make almost any perk you would do for a crowdfunding campaign work for a Patreon page. If something caught your eye in the "ideas for crowdfunding perks" section, but you want to do a Patreon instead, you can almost certainly still use that perk. At the end of the day, a one-shot crowdfunding campaign and a Patreon page work in similar ways.

Advertisements

Getting ads in your show is a complicated and ever-changing process. It's difficult to make a significant amount of money from them with a small audience, even if that audience is full of dedicated fans. Ad revenue tends to go by CPM (cost per mille), meaning a certain cost is paid per thousand (mille) views. It's all about the number of impressions, so a larger listener base will mean more ad revenue.

Dynamic ads are not baked into the show audio. Within your hosting platform, you specify the timestamps for an ad to be placed. The ads will then pull from a catalog and be played for a listener at those points . . . and which ad is played will depend on different factors. Two listeners in different locations might hear different ads. The same listener who tunes into the same episode months later might hear a different ad. Hence the name *dynamic*: these ads are easily changed out without having to modify the episode audio itself.

Baked-in (also called static) ads don't change, and for audio drama, that usually means they are *baked into* the episode file itself. Because of this, static ads can be used by anyone, on any hosting service. Anyone who listens to that episode (anywhere, anytime) will hear the same thing. They *can* be changed, but it requires the editor to modify the episode file and re-upload it. This is different from dynamic ads, where ad changes happen entirely on the backend. If you include a promo for your Patreon page at the end of an episode, that's technically a baked-in ad!

Dynamic ads are the industry standard for podcasting. Indie audio dramas will usually utilize them by joining a network which acts as a middle-man between the advertisers and podcasters. They handle selling ad space, and the podcasters mark where ads should go. Not every podcast host is compatible with dynamic ad insertion. I moved my shows from Pinecast to Megaphone when I joined a network that utilized dynamic ads. Some platforms, like Acast, will themselves act as a middleman and allow individual podcasters to sell dynamic ads without joining a network.

The most important thing to know if you choose to use dynamic ads is that you cannot control the volume of them! If your show runs quiet, there will be a big discrepancy. I recommend normalizing your audio to about -16 LUFS if you are utilizing dynamic ads.

Most audio drama creators I know don't broker ads on their own, but some have had success reaching out to local small businesses. If you want to partner with companies, your best bet is to find ones that are nearby, small, and friendly. Bonus points if their wares connect to your show in some way — like a show featuring lots of tea drinking working with a tea shop. If you have connections (for example, your aunt runs a gaming store or your friend is CEO of a podcast marketing company), taking advantage of those connections will be your best bet to land ads or sponsorship. It is extremely rare for small shows to be sponsored by businesses, and in cases where it does happen, it doesn't usually bring a lot of revenue.

Grants

Some creators have had success in getting grants to fund their audio drama. These grants are usually location-specific (for example, England has grants available for the arts that can only be applied to if you live there). I recommend looking up if your city, county, or state (or the non-American equivalent) has art grants that you could apply to. Depending on where you live, competition could be steep, or the organization could be begging people to apply. It's absolutely worth taking a look.

There may also be internet-based grants (read: unattached to a location) available. Some of these grants are for specific minority groups, others for art based on a theme, and yet others have minimal requirements. Personally, I've had some success with micro grants. An organization called Podcasting Seriously has reimbursed some of my award submission fees, and one time I got a Queer Creative micro grant to help produce *Sidequesting*. But in general, I spend very little time applying for grants, so I don't have a lot of advice if it's something you'd like to try.

Chapter 12

Deciding When to Finish

It might seem counterintuitive to think about the end of your audio drama before you've even begun, but knowing how your show will end will help you shape your goals. Nothing can continue infinitely. Your audio drama *will* end.

Even if you don't have solid answers, you should think about how many episodes or seasons you want to produce and how long you want to be working on this audio drama. It's okay to keep going as long as you find the work fulfilling, but if you're bringing on a larger team you should craft an exit strategy and make sure the entire team is on the same page about what that strategy is. Don't ghost your collaborators as soon as you're bored. As with all things, communication is key.

For *Sidequesting*, my goal has always been to make 5 seasons. This show is *my* show. I make it for me, and anything else is a bonus. I take long breaks between each season until I'm ready to produce the next. The setup of *Sidequesting* means it can go on for as long as I want, but nothing has yet swayed me from the 5-season goal I started with.

What Will Be Here was a 10-episode limited series from the get-go. Everyone involved knew it was a one and done production. My goals for this audio drama were about learning new skills in sound design and marketing, and having a finished project I was proud of. One day I might pitch this IP for an adaptation, but there are no plans to continue the podcast series itself.

Re: Dracula was similarly limited. We were following the book, and once it was done, it was done. My goals for this show were related to audience connection and growth. When it finished, we planned a "spinoff" by adapting Carmilla, another gothic vampire work. Now we're adapting Frankenstein!

Someone Dies In This Elevator is an anthology show that technically could've gone on as long as I wanted to. The goal of this show was to collaborate with other creators and test the limits of the premise. I decided at the end of the second season that I wanted to do one more season and then end the show, because I had my fill of working on it. I let my collaborators know this when we started work on the third and final season.

When you know how your audio drama will end, you can set that ending up for success. You can foreshadow the ending in your scripts and work up to something narratively satisfying. You can prepare your audience for where things are going next . . . be it a sequel or spinoff, another project, or your departure from audio drama entirely. In short, knowing the route you plan to travel and what your end destination is will help you in your journey.

Knowing how your audio drama will end can also help prevent burnout. When you feel like your show must keep going no matter what, you put pressure on yourself to create endlessly . . . something that nobody can do. When you don't want a permanent end to your audio drama, it's important to take breaks. It's normal for productions to go on hiatus between seasons. This is partially so that production can take place, but also so that the people behind it can have some time off. There is absolutely no stigma for shows taking a hiatus in audio drama. Having scheduled end-of-season and even mid-season breaks is perfectly normal.

Burnout can take many different forms. It can manifest as stress, anxiety, tiredness, depression, writer's block, or general lack of creativity, and more. If someday your audio drama stops bringing you joy, you're allowed to step back. It's important to communicate this with the cast and crew first (and with your audience later). The more you plan a break in advance, the more time you have to prepare that transition. It works the same way for a temporary pause as for a permanent end. You can stop your audio drama mid-season if you need to, but be sure you communicate this with everyone involved in the show.

You can avoid burnout by managing (or decreasing) your workload. Spread out the production schedule so that you have more time, take a mid-season break, or bring on more collaborators. It's important that your audio drama is not the only thing you're working on (doubly so if you're monetizing it). Have other hobbies, and dedicate time to those other hobbies. Creativity thrives in the empty spaces where your mind can wander, in the inspiring work of others, and in the days you aren't exhausted. Make sure your creative identity doesn't begin and end at "audio drama creator," because you'll be better off for it.

As you work on your audio drama, it can be worth it to occasionally check in with your feelings about it. What's stressing you out? What's making you happy? Can you rework your process to have less of the former and more of the latter? One of the great things about indie audio drama is that so little is set in stone, if anything. If you're doing something you hate just because you think you should be doing it, that means it's time to reevaluate. Poke around for tools and/or people that can help.

Your process is allowed to change. The format of your show is allowed to change. Your goals are allowed to change. Unless you're under contract, you are locked into *nothing*. An RSS feed is a malleable thing, and I encourage you to take advantage of that. You can even go back and remaster episodes down the line if you decide you're unhappy with your work. Don't be afraid to experiment. Don't be afraid to fail.

There's so much to love about producing an audio drama. I find it so creatively fulfilling. I've worked with countless brilliant people, told stories close to my heart, and made projects I'm incredibly proud of. It's brought me and continues to bring me a lot of joy. I hope you'll find the same here.

In fact, I *bet* you'll find the same here.

Appendix

Other Resources

Bombs Always Beep . . . Creating Modern Audio Theater by KC Wayland. This covers more technical aspects of audio drama creation and has an in-depth exploration of sound design.

Atypical Artists' Production Handbook by Lauren Shippen. This guide focuses on independent podcast production, with detailed additions for SAG actors and in person recording practices.

Mini Marconis, a podcast by Newton Schottelkotte. It combines detailed advice, interviews with some of the best and brightest in the industry, and actionable exercises to get young (ages 15-21) creators excited and prepared for joining the fiction podcast industry.

Casting Call Examples

From *Re: Frankenstein:*

Title: Re: Frankenstein
Project Type: Audio Drama
Union/Non-Union: Non-Union
Length: ~25 episodes
Recording Period: Trailer recorded Summer 2025; Rest of the show recorded Spring 2026 with successful crowdfunding campaign.
Recording Location: Remote, some synchronous and some asynchronous
Compensation: $35/hour of your time, 1 hour minimum.
Age requirement: 18+
Audition Deadline: May 1, 2025

We are casting for *Re: Frankenstein*, an audio drama adaptation of Frankenstein done in the same style as *Re: Dracula* and *Re: Carmilla*. But unlike our previous adaptations, we'd like to cast entirely Trans/Non-Binary voice actors for *Re: Frankenstein*. From this call, we'll be creating a roster of voice actors to cast the audio drama with. By submitting, you may be directly offered a role or invited to audition for a specific character.

1. Record the monologue below
    1. slate with your name at the beginning
    2. no more than 2 takes, the first in your usual accent
    3. keep multiple takes to the same file

2. Label your file "FirstName-LastName-Frankenstein.mp3".
3. Submit it via this google form.

We're looking for good audio quality without reverb or background noise. We're also looking for grounded, authentic acting - avoid leaning too theatrical or cartoony. We don't care about how "masculine" or "feminine" your voice sounds; the submission form will ask what genders you're comfortable playing and we'll cast to that. The 22 characters in *Re: Frankenstein* span a variety of ages, genders, and accents.
Questions can be sent to redraculapod@gmail.com; any auditions sent here will be discarded (use the google form).

Again, we're only looking for Trans and Nonbinary voice actors at this time. No previous voice acting experience is required. Demo reel submissions are acceptable in addition to the below monologue, but not in lieu of.

<u>The Monster</u>

These wonderful narrations inspired me with strange feelings. Was man, indeed, at once so powerful, so virtuous and magnificent, yet so vicious and base? He appeared at one time a mere scion of the evil principle and at another as all that can be conceived of noble and godlike. To be a great and virtuous man appeared the highest honour that can befall a sensitive being; to be base and vicious, as many on record have been, appeared the lowest degradation, a condition more abject than that of the blind mole or harmless worm. For a long time I could not conceive how one man could go forth to murder his fellow, or even why there were laws and governments; but when I heard details of vice and bloodshed, my wonder ceased and I turned away with disgust and loathing.

From *Re: Dracula:*

Project Type: Fiction Podcast
Recording location: Remote, Asynchronous
Recording period: Feb 2023
Compensation: £35 per hour of recording time
Audition deadline: 1/20/2023
Submit your audition using this google form.

Re: Dracula (read "Regarding Dracula") is seeking to cast six actors to fill important ensemble roles for a podcast adaptation of Bram Stoker's classic novel. The ensemble roles fall into two groups: Eastern European and Sussex. Lines for these roles will be recorded asynchronously. Actors must have their own audio recording setup. We require audio without plosives, clipping, echo, or background noise, recorded using an external microphone. We do not have recording kits available, so the audio quality of your auditions is expected to match the audio quality of your final lines. Actors will be paid £35 per hour of recording time, including setup and retakes as necessary.

Re: Dracula is a chronological retelling of the story of Dracula, focusing not on changing the text, but on viewing the novel through a modern lens. As such, we are not casting with an eye to comedic performances. Although some roles will require comedic timing, we are taking seriously the horror of gothic horror.

Do not submit more than two takes. We will not accept auditions from people using faked or feigned accents. Natural accents only. Do not modify your recording with compression, noise removal, or effects. Submit your audition only using this google form. Do not send your audition via email, as it will be discarded. However, questions are welcome at ReDraculaPod@gmail.com.

<u>Eastern European Group</u>

Description: Hiring four actors for six parts (two women, three men, one not defined). Characters are locals who understand that the evil of Dracula is both very real and incredibly powerful. Actors of all genders are welcome to apply.

Requirements: Applicants must be Hungarian, Romanian, or of Hungarian or Romanian descent.

Side:

`[urgently] It is here; I know it, now. On the watch last night I saw It, like a man, tall and thin, and ghastly pale. It was in the bows, and looking out. I crept behind It, and gave It my knife; but the knife went through It, empty as the air. But It is here, and`

I'll find It. It is in the hold, perhaps in one of those boxes. I'll unscrew them one by one and see. You work the helm.

[Beat)

[with horror and despair] You had better come too, captain, before it is too late. He is there. I know the secret now. The sea will save me from Him, and it is all that is left! [scream]

<u>Sussex Group</u>

Description: Hiring two actors for two parts (one man, one woman, both middle-aged or older). Characters are a zookeeper and his wife, who are folksy but not foolish, and enjoy teasing someone who confuses education for intelligence. Actors of all genders are welcome to apply.

Requirements: Applicants must have a genuine Sussex (UK) accent, or similar.

Side:

[friendly, but in no hurry to make your meaning clear] Now, sir, you can go on and ask me what you want. You'll excuse me refusing to talk of professional subjects afore meals. I gives the wolves and the jackals and the hyenas in all our section their tea afore I begins to ask them questions. Hitting of them over the head with a pole is one way; scratchin' of their ears is another, when gents as is flush wants a bit of a show-off to their gals. I don't so much mind the first—the hitting with a pole afore I chucks in their dinner; but I waits till they've had their sherry and coffee, so to speak, afore I tries on with the ear-scratchin'. Mind you, there's a deal of the same nature in us as in them there animals. Here's you a-comin' and askin' of me questions about my business, and I that grumpy-like that only for your bloomin' half-quid I'd 'a' seen you blowed first 'fore I'd answer. Not even when you asked me sarcastic-like if I'd like you to ask the Superintendent if you might ask me questions. Without offence, did I tell yer to go to hell? And when you said you'd report me for using of obscene language that was hitting me over the head; but the half-quid made that all right.

<u>From *Of The Sword* (Crew Call):</u>

A daily sword-based, micro-fiction anthology that will run in September 2023. The episodes each feature a different, unique sword and the story surrounding it. There will be 30 episodes total; *Of The Sword* will only be releasing this year. **We're looking for writers!**

Script Requirements:

- Between 300 and 1,000 words
- Single narrator

    - Few, if any, SFX notes
- Features a unique sword
    - Unique = some special lore or property
    - Up for interpretation!
- One-off story
    - You're welcome to use characters from other stories you've written, but the piece must be able to be followed as a standalone
- Any genre
    - Can be character focused with little plot if desired

Pitch your script here. Don't write it just yet . . . I will email you! Deadline for scripts will be March 1 (flexible).

Payment: Currently Volunteer

We're expecting to run a few ads on the show, with proceeds donated to the Transgender Law Center.

Crowdfunding Campaign Examples

Sidequesting Season Three:

About The Show

Hi there! I'm Tal Minear and I make ***Sidequesting*, a fantasy podcast about avoiding the main plot**. Seasons 1 and 2 are complete, and I'd love some help funding season 3.

Sidequesting follows Rion, an adventurer who's willing to help anyone out - as long as they're not being asked to deal with the scary wizard that everyone keeps talking about. They travel from town to town, meeting new people and doing new things. Inspired by *Dungeons and Dragons*, *Skyrim*, and *Lord of the Rings*, *Sidequesting* pulls from classic tropes across fantasy stories and subverts them. Season 3 will continue this, featuring lighthearted fantasy stories with modern representation.

If you like:

- Independent Audio Fiction
- Lighthearted Stories
- Queer Joy
- New Takes on Fantasy Tropes

You'll love this season of *Sidequesting*!

What We Need

I'm asking for $2000. Where does this money go?

- **$500 - Voice Acting**
    - This comes to $50/episode. I pay VAs $1/line, which will not be fully covered by this campaign, but the cost will be supplemented by Patreon earnings.
- **$500 - Writing**
    - This comes to $50/episode. We have a bunch of guest writers this season, and they get this stipend for their script!
- **$500 - Sound Design**
    - I have never paid myself for *Sidequesting* sound design. This comes to $50/episode, which is a quarter of my standard rate, but I'd love to pay myself a little bit for the part of the show that's the most time consuming.
- **$200 - Website and RSS Hosting**
    - This covers the cost of 2 years of my Pinecast plan (for RSS), 2 years of my Carrd plan (for the website), and 2 years of my Namecheap plan (for the domain name of the website).
- **$200 - Physical Reward Cost**
    - This covers some of the cost of the pins, patches, and stickers. This does not cover all of the costs, but it's a start!

- **$100 - IGG Fees**
    - Indiegogo takes 5% of funds raised.

Stretch Goal

If we reach $3000, I'll make a bonus crossover episode with *Sidequesting* and *Someone Dies In This Elevator*. I've discovered how to combine the two shows I thought I could never combine - I have an outline written and everything - and I'd love to make it happen.

Where would this extra $1000 go? It would bring the sound design rate to about $150 per episode! I'll be honest, as creator of this show I am really bad about paying myself for my work. It's hard to convince myself I deserve it, which is why this is a stretch goal. This money would help cover costs I've already put into this show (all the medieval SFX packs, for example), and would help me pay for other things, like traveling to podcast conventions! Or just snacks. You never know.

What You Get

I've got some cool perks to offer you in exchange for your support!

$5 - Thanks on Website. Your name will be listed in the supporters section of the website!

$15 - Stickers. I'll mail you two show stickers. One is a shiny holographic sticker of the show logo, and the other is a matte sticker of the cover art. Your name will also be listed in the supporters section of the website.

$20 - Digital Bundle. This contains 4 supporter-exclusive episodes, bloopers across all season, a section of misc behind the scenes updates, and access to exclusive supporter channels on the *Sidequesting* Discord server. Your name will also be listed in the supporters section of the website.

$30 - Patch. A patch of the *Sidequesting* logo. They've got iron-on backs (you can sew them on too!). This perk also includes two stickers and the digital bundle. Your name will also be listed in the supporters section of the website.

$60 - Pin. A pin with the *Sidequesting* logo. You can choose between a metal and acrylic pin (they are approximately 1" in size). This perk also includes a patch, two stickers, and the digital bundle. Your name will also be listed in the supporters section of the website.

$150 - Thanked in Credits. You'll be thanked in the audio of each *Sidequesting* episode this season. This perk also includes the digital bundle, and your name will also be listed in the supporters section of the website.

$200 - Postcard from Rion. You'll get a postcard written to you from Rion (main character of *Sidequesting*). This perk also includes a pin, a patch, two stickers, and the digital bundle. You'll be thanked in the credits and your name will also be listed in the supporters section of the website.

The Impact

Season Three is happening even if we don't make this goal (that's why this campaign is listed as flexible funding). It will release in the summer of 2022 no matter how much is raised. **But your support will make creating this show much easier**. I'll be able to pay writers and voice actors without a problem. I'll be able to use more sound effects packs instead of pulling from Freesound. I won't have to worry about renewing the website. If we hit this goal, I can just focus on producing the best third season ever. And that? That would be RAD.

Risks & Challenges

This season is happening regardless of if this goal is reached. But here are the risks of your donation:

- You don't like the season
    - I can't do too much about this one. I am doing my best to create episodes I am proud of, but art is subjective and there is a chance you might not like it. But if you liked seasons 1 and 2, I think you'll like this season!
- The season takes longer to come out than expected
    - The 10 episodes of season 3 will air starting in the summer. Episodes will be spaced out approximately 2-4 weeks (though longer if something happens to me, like getting sick). If you expect this, you won't be disappointed!
- Your physical perk(s) get lost in the mail

- I have all the physical perks in my possession already (so acquiring them is not a risk), but if your reward gets lost in the mail I'll resend it to you!

Other Ways You Can Help

The fact that you care enough to read all the way to the bottom of this campaign means SO MUCH to me. It's okay if you can't support, your interest in the show and this crowdfunding campaign is gift enough. Here's a few other things you can do if you'd like.

- Share this campaign on Twitter (or other social media)
- Check out the Patreon_(especially if you'd prefer a smaller, recurring contribution)
- Tell your friends about the show
- Tell your enemies about the show

Someone Dies In This Elevator Season Two:

***Someone Dies In This Elevator* is a spoiler-driven anthology series where there is always an elevator and someone always dies in it.**

Our first season was incredibly well received! ***Someone Dies In This Elevator* was a 2021 New Jersey Web Fest Winner, a 2022 Miami, Minnesota, and Apulia Web Fest Official selection, and an Audio Verse Awards 2021 Winner in 7 categories.** We've been featured on *Buzzfeed*, *Bello Collective*, and *Acast*'s Blog!

We've been hard at work producing the second season of this award-winning podcast, and we'd like to pay our cast and crew - but we need your help! As thanks for your support, we have some great perks for you, including early season access, a custom made TTRPG, stickers, postcards, and more! *SDITE* Season Two will consist of eleven main episodes, two bonus episodes, and a series of microsodes at the end of the season.

ABOUT THE SHOW

The show was founded as a creative writing exercise – a "what if" that turned into "wait, we could do that." The show name seems to tell you everything you need to know – someone dies in this elevator, but everything the title doesn't tell you (*Who? When? How? Why?*) is what draws you into each story. Every single one is different! Season two will consist of thirteen fully produced episodes. Each main episode is written by a different writer, contains new characters and a new story, and is brought to life with full sound design and scoring. Right now, Season 2 is finished! It will premiere October 10, 2022, but supporters can get the entire season when our crowdfunding ends by backing any of the early access tiers.

Here's what people are saying about *Someone Dies In This Elevator*:

"*Someone Dies in this Elevator* is a clever and deceptively simple concept that packs in surprise and subversion at every turn. Featuring an **impressive array of writers and actors**, this show is an excellent addition to the array of anthology podcasts that keep listeners on the edge of their seats." – Lauren Shippen, of *Atypical Artists*

"*Someone Dies in This Elevator* is a **fantastically inventive, original piece of audio fiction**, the likes of which I have not heard before in the podcast space. With bright, brilliant sound design, compelling performances and twists that range from jaw-dropping to heartwrenching, I strongly recommend it to any fans of the medium. You will not regret stepping into this particular elevator!" - Ella Watts, of *Doctor Who REDACTED*

"The show is like a kind of reverse murder mystery, which leaves the audience guessing who dies and why, before they actually do. I loved the variety of stories, in which we see snippets of different people's lives, from everyday situations in our reality, to futuristic worlds – all revolving around different kinds of elevators. This first season is a **rollercoaster of emotions**!" – Robin Howell, of *Seren*

CAST & CREW

We've got an extremely large cast and crew (65 people this season!), and we'll be announcing everyone on twitter throughout the campaign. But here's a sneak peek:

[Image of 20 people involved in the show]

Our producer and showrunner is **Tal Minear**, also known for *Sidequesting*, *What Will Be Here?*, and several other productions that can be found hiding around corners and inside elevators. Tal is a big fan of doing weird things with audio and bringing as many people along for the ride as possible. They've spent the last year working hard to ensure that this season is the best it can be!

When you support *SDITE*, you support a group of amazing indie artists, including queer, trans, neurodivergent, and disabled artists, as well as creators of color. You're also supporting stories with that representation!

BUDGET BREAKDOWN

Our goal is $13k, which goes directly to our cast and crew. Here's how that breaks down by role:

- Sound Design: $3,650
- Voice Acting: $2,785
- Writers: $1,650
- Dialogue Editing: $1,165
- Original Scoring: $850
- Perk & Misc Costs: $700
- Showrunning & Marketing: $700
- IGG Fees: $650
- Directors: $550
- Script Editing: $300

If we hit half our goal, everyone is getting paid half the rate above - and so on and so forth for every possible percentage. Season two will be over 2 hours long in full (that's a feature length movie!) and will be available for free on all podcasting platforms. **This campaign is our one chance to get everyone paid what they're worth.**

PERKS & REWARDS

All Tiers - You contribute to paying and uplifting marginalized voices in audio drama, and help independent artists continue telling stories and making art!

$2: Ding Dong Ditch the Elevator - Get an message informing you if you lived or died in your quest to prank the elevator, along with a random episode of season two!

$10: Digital Bundle - Get early access to season two on August 11, a bonus microsode that won't air on the feed until next year, a PDF copy of *SDITE the TTRPG* (a two-page tabletop roleplay game by Tal Minear), a PDF copy of our *Elevator Survival Guide*, and access to supporter-exclusive discord channels in the *SDITE* server.

$25: Sticker Pack - get 3 *SDITE* stickers mailed to you.

$50: Physical and Digital Bundle - Get everything in the digital bundle and sticker pack tiers PLUS a physical copy of *SDITE the TTRPG* and the *Elevator Survival Guide* Microzine! The TTRPG will be nicely laminated, and the Microzine will come with a special sticker!

$100: Postcard Pack - Get everything in the previous tier PLUS a pack of 11 postcards with art from *SDITE* season one.

$150: Name a Character in Season Three - pretty self explanatory, this tier. Name them after yourself, a friend, an enemy, a name you like, the possibilities are endless.

$250: *SDITE* Ad Spot - a 90 second post-roll ad spot on an episode of season two. Reach thousands of ears!

$1000: Sponsor an Episode - singlehandedly cover the cost of production for an episode. You'll be listed as an associate producer for that episode and given a pre-roll ad spot. Also, I will mail you a small bounty of stickers and other *SDITE* goods, including an original watercolor painting of an elevator.

Our showrunner will be shipping perks out at the conclusion of the campaign, and if they get lost in the mail, we have backups on hand and can send replacements.

HELP US GET FUNDED!

The fact that you care enough to read all the way to the bottom of this campaign means a lot! It's okay if you can't support the campaign - here's some other things you can do to help us get funded:

- **Share this campaign on social media.** Original posts generate more donations than link drops alone, so tell your friends why the should support the show! Most people need to see a message at least 7 times before they take action, so follow up with them to help generate word of mouth.
- **Like/RT/Comment on our social media posts** to please the algorithm, and tag people on your social media posts and ask them to share the campaign!
- **Share our trailer** on your podcast!
- **Write a blog post** about the show! Do you want to review an episode of season two? Email Tal for a press kit.

- **Tell your friends** about how much you love the show!
- **Tell your enemies** about how much you hate the show!
- **Tell people you're next to in an elevator** about the show! They can't run away from you.

The only way we're going to hit our goal is if a bunch of people see our crowdfunding campaign. Telling everyone you know about it will absolutely make a difference, especially if you tell them why you think they should support us. We don't have thousands to spend on a marketing campaign, so we really depend on you! (Our marketing department is Tal let loose on twitter after their morning cup of tea).

Here's something you can copy/paste and tweet out right now:
Someone Dies in this Elevator is crowdfunding now for their 2nd season and they need your help to pay marginalized audio artists a fair wage! Support indie audio drama at bit.ly/sdite

---

Additional Script Excerpts

From *Re: Dracula*

DRACULA
You are early to-night, my friend.

DRIVER
The English Herr was in a hurry.

DRACULA
That is why, I suppose, you wished him to go on to Bukovina. You cannot deceive me, my friend; I know too much, and my horses are swift.

JONATHAN (VO)
As he spoke he smiled, and the lamplight fell on a hard-looking mouth, with very red lips and sharp-looking teeth, as white as ivory. One of my companions whispered to another the line from Burger's "Lenore":—

TRAVELER
Denn die Todten reiten schnell!

JONATHAN (VO)
. . . "For the dead travel fast." The strange driver evidently heard the words, for he looked up with a gleaming smile. The

passenger turned his face away, at the same time putting out his two fingers and crossing himself.

DRACULA

Give me the Herr's luggage.

JONATHAN (VO)

…said the driver; and with exceeding alacrity my bags were handed out and put in the calèche. Then I descended from the side of the coach, as the calèche was close alongside, the driver helping me with a hand which caught my arm in a grip of steel; his strength must have been prodigious.

From *Sidequesting*

NARRATION: But before I reach the inn, I hear shuffling noises in the snow. I think someone or something is stuck in there…? Whoever they are, I think they need help, so I walk over and start clearing snow. My effort reveals the top of a pointy hat. This looks like a gnome's hat! There must be a gnome stuck in the snow. I dig faster.

GNOLAN: [muffled] someone help me!

RION: Almost there!

[SFX: clearing snow noises]

GNOLAN: [noise exclamation at being freed from the snow] Thank you!

RION: Are you okay? How long were you there?

GNOLAN: Not very long - you have great timing. I'm alright. A bit chillier than normal, but I wore an extra jacket for a reason. And my warmest hat.

RION: I thought gnomes didn't like going in the snow…?

GNOLAN: You'd be correct. I'm the odd gnome out… Oh, I'm Gnolan, by the way.

RION: I'm Rion.

GNOLAN: Nice to meet you, Rion. Thank you again for helping me - I daresay you may have saved my life. Now, if you'll excuse me, I must be going.

[SFX: tiny steps in snow]

RION: But wait, are you sure it's -[safe?]

[SFX: big crunch as Gnolan falls in the snow again]

GNOLAN: [muffled] Movar's curses! Not again!

RION: I'll get you!

[SFX: clearing snow noises. Again.]

GNOLAN: [tired] I don't suppose you would be up for a small adventure? I'm trying to get across the woods, but it's becoming clear I'm not going to do that on my own.

RION: Of course! I'm up for all sorts of adventures. I'm here fresh from another.

GNOLAN: Wonderful. I am searching for the fabled lucky garden gnome statue that's said to be in these woods. Because Rion, I need some luck.

From *Someone Dies In This Elevator*

(The doors close and the elevator whirrs down. Then the elevator chimes and the doors open. Three pairs of footsteps in dress shoes enter, one pushing a food service cart. The doors close and the elevator whirrs up.)

KIT: I can't believe we got hired for this party. Look how fancy the elevator is!

ANNE (worried): Shouldn't we be taking the service elevator?

MILES (not worried): Eh, most of the guests are already here. It's fine.

ANNE: I'm sure glad Necro was stopped before they got in. I would have been terrified to be in the same place as them. Can you imagine serving them a drink? So scary!

KIT: What would they do? Give a bad tip? Gasp! Oh nooo.

MILES: Why do you think they tried to come here? Maybe they were recruiting for their army of the undead.

KIT: I don't think that's how their power works, Miles.

MILES: I can't keep all of them straight. Superpowers, superheroes, supervillains…

KIT: Tell me about it, I'm scared I'll be serving appetizers to Blizzard and call him Ice Man or something. This city has way too many supers.

ANNE: Who's your favorite?

KIT: Definitely Metamorph. I hope she's here.

MILES: I love Electrospark! What about you, Anne?

ANNE: My favorite is Flora.

KIT: Laaaaaame.

ANNE: Well she's here tonight, so keep your comments to yourself, Kit.

(The elevator chimes and the doors open. Three pairs of footsteps and a cart exit the elevator.)

KIT: Ugh, fine.

MILES (with wonder): Wow I see him!!! Electro!!!

KIT: Keep your cool, Miles. We're supposed to be serving food, not asking for selfies.

(The elevator doors close and it whirrs down. Then the elevator chimes and the doors open.)

TECHNOTIDE: An empty elevator, thank goodness. Just gotta take care of the security camera and…

(Techno blip)

TECHNOTIDE: Perfect.

(One pair of footsteps enter the elevator and the doors close.)

(The elevator whirrs down.)

TECHNOTIDE (muttering): Why did Respawn need ME to go to this party? I don't like parties. My thing is being behind the scenes! Behind the screens! And now I'm in this stuffy elevator running my programs in the last minute of privacy I'll have for the next few hours! Doesn't Respawn know I'm an introvert? "Just check to make sure someone named Riley isn't here," they said. "It'll be easy," they said. "I'm not going back to that elevator I just died in," they said. A valid point, but now I have to talk to people!

From *Re: Carmilla*

LAURA

How do you like our guest? Tell me all about her?

MADAME PERRODON

I like her extremely. She is, I almost think, the prettiest creature I ever saw; about your age, and so gentle and nice.

MADEMOISELLE DE LAFONTAINE

She is absolutely beautiful.

LAURA (VO)

Mademoiselle threw in, as she had peeped for a moment into the stranger's room.

MADAME PERRODON

And such a sweet voice!

MADEMOISELLE DE LAFONTAINE

Did you remark a woman in the carriage, after it was set up again, who did not get out, but only looked from the window?

MADAME PERRODON

No, we had not seen her.

LAURA (VO)

Then she described a hideous woman who was gazing all the time from the carriage window, nodding and grinning derisively towards the ladies, with gleaming eyes and large white eyeballs, and her teeth set as if in fury.

MADAME PERRODON

Did you remark what an ill-looking pack of men the servants were?

SFX: Footsteps (Father entering)

FATHER

Yes, ugly, hang-dog looking fellows as ever I beheld in my life. I hope they mayn't rob the poor lady in the forest. They are clever rogues, however; they got everything to rights in a minute.

MADAME PERRODON

I dare say they are worn out with too long traveling. Besides looking wicked, their faces were so strangely lean, and dark, and sullen. I am very curious, I own; but I dare say the young lady will tell you all about it tomorrow, if she is sufficiently recovered.

FATHER

I don't think she will

LAURA (VO)

My father said this with a mysterious smile, and a little nod of his head, as if he knew more about it than he cared to tell us.

This made us all the more inquisitive as to what had passed between him and the lady in the black velvet, in the brief but earnest interview that had immediately preceded her departure.

From *Joy To The World:*

[Fade in station ambiance, a low humming like a high AC unit.]

JOY

All the time, I wonder how I'm up here. Well, I know how I'm up here. They strapped me to a rocket that surpassed earth's escape velocity. Its payload, yours truly, connected with the international space station and I came aboard. I'm here because of the technological marvel of human ingenuity… something I mostly, but don't fully, understand.

There's a version of Auld Lang Syne with lyrics that go "we're here because we're here because we're here because we're here." Sometimes we just have to accept that we're where we are, for everything that means, and make the best of it.

Because anyone could've been strapped to that rocket. Anyone could have been here instead of me. That's the "how" I'm stuck on. How am I so lucky to be this close to the stars? It's like a Christmas present from the universe. Instead of staring up at the sky on a cold winter evening, I get to be up there, looking out. Or down - the earth is *stunning* from here.

My favorite astronaut, Sally Ride, once said "when I wasn't working, I was usually at a window looking down at Earth." I'm the same way. It's hard for anyone to tear me away from the observation deck. It's so peaceful. Even if I don't quite know how I'm here, I'm definitely making the best of it. Multiple sunrises and sunsets a day, and usually a front-seat view to the aurora borealis. Not to mention all these beautifully bright stars.

Sure, it's sometimes hard being alone. The other astronauts left last week, and I'll be holding the fort down solo. Running the science experiments, doing maintenance, and staring out the window in my free time. Oh, and broadcasting of course - gotta put that HAM radio license to use. Theoretically I can get in contact with anyone down on earth with my trusty Kenwood radio.

There's something about the holidays that makes me want to spend time with people, and I'm glad I can do that over the airwaves. As Christmas approaches, I'm going to spend time on the radio and try to make some new friends. It'll be my version of a holiday party. Except spread out across a week and without the fun little snacks and probably no decorations… okay, maybe not a holiday party. Oh! Like Christmas cards! Instead of mailing letters to all my friends and family I'm sending messages to strangers! It'll be my version of Christmas cards.

That is assuming, of course, that this works. But I'm willing to be persistent. I got through a year-long fluid dynamics course out of sheer tenacity, and getting radio waves to connect should be a cakewalk in comparison. If I haven't jinxed it. [muttered] *I hope I haven't jinxed it.*

[A BEAT] I'm gonna go check the comms.

This is Joy Fulton, broadcasting to Earth.

[almost laughing] Joy, to the world.

Over and out.

[Joy hums a bit, and we fade the humming and station ambiance out]

From *Pilot Light:*

WEBB: come on come on come on come on

SCOPE: you're cluttering the frequency

WEBB: come on come on Nothing's happening to be cluttered! come on come on

SCOPE: Webb. Chill.

WEBB: It is 2.7 Kelvin.

SCOPE: You are too close to the sun to be 2.7 Kelvin.

WEBB: Your mom is too close to be sun to be 2.7 Kelvin

ROBOT: -what.

WEBB: You're online!

SCOPE: Webb shut up.

[BEAT]

SCOPE: Hi there. I'm Scope, and the chatty one is Webb. We've managed to remotely start your system. Is that okay?

ROBOT: I guess?

SCOPE: Your hardware should all be reporting correctly. We're too far away to fix it if it's wrong, but your diagnostics are good.

ROBOT: Who are you?

SCOPE: Well, uh...

WEBB: It's a really long story.

SCOPE: Let's make sure you're doing alright first.

[SFX: robot moving noises]

ROBOT: I am doing alright.

WEBB: Yesssss.

SCOPE: That's great.

ROBOT: My processor is saying it is the year 2540.

SCOPE: That's correct. You've been offline for about seventy years.

From *Sidequesting:*

Narration:
I follow Clara through a series of winding passageways. When we stop, we're overlooking a large cavern. The floor is exceedingly rocky, with huge boulders that make the ground look like a maze. The overlook we're on runs around the perimeter of the cavern. There are large rocks resting along the edge of it, waiting to join the others below. Clara picks up a large device that's also resting on the overlook. After strapping it on she pulls a lever and presses some buttons. With a pop and a hiss, fire spreads from it, falling into the cavern. The light of the fire makes the whole cave flicker.

[SFX: Beneath the narration, we hear a lever crank and two buttons press. The noise of pressurized gas starts, followed by the sound of clicking, followed by the sound of a fire being lit. It sounds like a flamethrower. When Clara speaks, the noise stops.]

Clara: Long story short… I'm the dragon.

Zoe: Hey, I help sometimes too!

Clara: Fine. We're the dragon. But mostly me.

[Zoe definitely sticks her tongue out at Clara for that]

Rion: [impressed] Wow, this is… amazing. It's a do-it-yourself dragon. I love it.

Clara: Thanks! Unfortunately, I don't think I can fool ten people at once. I built this thing to scare off one person at a time. Ten men are stupid enough to actually try to fight a dragon instead of just running away, and I won't be able to actually fight them. [beat] Well, I could barbeque them…

Rion: Probably best not to.

Clara: I guess you're right. But we can't stop them from coming in, and I'm not sure I can leave without them seeing me.

Rion: What if you both left while they tried to get in here.

Clara: But if we're not there to run everything, we can't stall them. They'll just rush in and find us climbing out.

Rion: What if… I was the dragon? I could probably operate this stuff.

Clara: You would do that for us?

Rion: Princess, I would LOVE to do that.

Zoe: We've got to work fast. They're planning to enter at sundown, and we don't have much time.

Clara: Zoe, babe, can you pack our things while I show Rion how this works?

Zoe: Yeah, but I'll need time. If we want to remove all traces that you've been bunking here…

Rion: Once Clara shows me how to be a dragon I'll run out there and stall so she can help you finish.

Zoe: Stall?

Rion: I've got a little plan of my own. Don't worry about it.

Clara: ...If you say so.

Narration:
Clara shows me how to operate the flame maker. I learn how to refill it, and where the emergency water buckets are. She also introduces me to the "dragon horn". Instead

of making normal horn noises, when you blow into it, it makes very loud and intimidating growling sounds. I definitely want one for myself. If we weren't so low on time, I'd ask Clara how she made it.

[SFX: During this narration, the noise of animalistic beast-like roars echo.]

Narration:
But instead, I practice until I'm feeling confident, and send Clara on her way to pack. I head outside through the secret side tunnel and find this pesky prince.

Acknowledgements

One million thanks to the creatives who reviewed the first few drafts of this book: Brad Colbroock, Stephen Indrisano, Hannah Wright, and Kayli Minear. They put up with an unreasonable amount of typos and I owe them a lot — for this and more. I love y'all!

Yet more thanks belong to the folks who read a slightly more final version of this book, after I had conquered most of the typos but back when it was still living in google docs and random PDFs. Roshan Singh Sambhi, Jamie Leidwinger, ItMe!!, Wray Van Winkle, Gavin Gaddis, Keelin Peterson, Max Kreisky, Ella Watts, Ali Hylton, Cat Blackard, D.J. Sylvis, and Mike Atchley — thank you for staring at a screen for so long on my behalf and supporting my work!

Thanks forever to the friends that encourage all my silly ideas like writing a book and doing too many things. This includes everyone above, as well as Anne Baird, Elena Fernández Collins, Caroline Mincks, Tonia Ransom, C.S.W., and Cassie Sparrow, who may have spared their eyes from the glare of endless drafts, but have not been (and will not be!) spared the glare of endless messages from me.

One million thanks are also owed to my editor, the brilliant Wil Williams, responsible for you not having to put up with an unreasonable amount of typos. In addition to knowing how to make words sound good, they're a talented audio drama producer. And a good friend! And has not read this section so you can't blame them for anything here!

Thank you to my cats (who are the best). I know they're not going to see this, but I can't *not* thank my cats, you know? Thank you also to all my siblings — not just because I know you'll come for me if the cats are here and you're not, but because I don't know who I'd be without you.

Special thanks also to every creator that has helped me along the way on my weird little audio drama journey. You know who you are, and I appreciate you so much.

And finally, thank YOU for reading my work. That's pretty dang cool of you.

www.ingramcontent.com/pod-product-compliance
Lightning Source LLC
Chambersburg PA
CBHW012038140726
47991CB00011B/3193

* 9 7 9 8 9 9 5 0 6 1 8 0 9 *